A single gargant can break a house beneath its
fists; in the Mortal Realms, this much is known
to even the poorest soot-child. Many a tale
is told of these monsters gobbling up unwary
travellers, smashing ironoaks into splinters
and shattering castle walls. The fact that they
gather in clans is rarely mentioned, for it is too
terrible to contemplate. If one of these towering
beasts spells ruin, a group of them is a walking
disaster. And they are evolving.

No more are the gargants simply bad-tempered
behemoths addled by too much meat and drink,
massive in stature but easily outwitted. Since
their godbeast father Behemat was slain by
Sigmar's hosts, they are on the warpath, a force
of ruination that crushes all before it. Worse
still, if the scholars of the free cities are to be
believed, they are getting larger. Some are so
vast they can simply step over the walls built to
keep them out, roaring at ear-splitting volume
as they feast on the fleshy morsels within.

To the gargant, the races of men, duardin and
aelf are weak. These gigantic oafs guffaw and
bellow as they grind such pipsqueaks underfoot,
relishing the feeling of breaking bones and
squishing flesh between their toes. They stamp
veteran warriors flat and kick armoured horses
into ordered shieldwalls just for the fun of
it. For them, battle is recreation. Intoxicated
with the thrill of their destructive crusade,
they spur each other on to ever greater feats
of destruction, revelling in the demise of every
regiment they crush and every prized warbeast
they tear apart.

The gargant of the past is gone. Now
come the Sons of Behemat, and they are
strength incarnate.

CONTENTS

PRODUCED BY THE WARHAMMER STUDIO
With thanks to The Faithful for their additional playtesting services.

Games Workshop Ltd., Willow Road, Lenton, Nottingham, NG7 2WS, United Kingdom
games-workshop.com

The sons of the godbeast Behemat stride fearlessly into a Flesh-eater Court's trap, crushing and squashing the ghouls of the Corpse Lakes as if they were trampling a field of rotten apples.

THE BEAST GARGANTUAN

Bellowing, stomping and crushing all before them, the Sons of Behemat are all but impossible to stop. Though they owe allegiance to no man, many are mercenaries, and fight all across the Mortal Realms. On the charge, a group of gargants can flatten a battleline whilst suffering only flesh wounds and the odd broken toe in return.

Gargants of many kinds exist throughout all the Mortal Realms. Feared across the lands for their sheer size and strength, they range from merely huge to absolutely colossal. Since the death of the zodiacal godbeast Behemat – who many gargants claim to be the father of their race – they have only grown larger still. Given that they have no natural predators, gargants act on their instincts and whims almost all the time. They usually fill their days by hunting, sleeping, eating people whole, drinking barrels of captured ale, sleeping again, belching, breaking wind at one another, and smashing other people's dwelling places for their own amusement. To stay in the path of a gargant is a very bad idea, for they see those smaller than themselves as playthings at best and, at worst, a quick snack.

Some gargants have hermetic existences, content to stay within their own wide-ranging territory. Others are constantly on the move, truly ravenous in their appetite for battle. When the titanic beings known as Mega-Gargants are on the warpath, a new focus spreads through gargant society – such as it is – that drives even the most reclusive of these massive louts into rampages of pitiless violence. They will sniff out prey no matter where it hides, and smash it to paste. Over time gargants gather together into war parties, following each other's footsteps until they become nigh unstoppable – a force of destruction so crude but effective they can smash a city to rubble, scatter an army to the winds, or topple one of the Great Wonders of the Mortal Realms.

Gargants are generally rather myopic when it comes to telling the smaller races apart. They pay little mind to the difference between one 'pipsqueak' and the next, regardless of the size of his hat or the shininess of his sword. Some of their number have learned to make alliances with the armies of the smaller races, for not only does this mean they are likely to get in a really good fight, they can also earn a larger share of the spoils of war as reward for their troubles. Yet for every paymaster that successfully bribes a gargant into his service – likely by standing on a cliff or tall building to ensure he is at least the same eye level – a dozen more are messily devoured. In general, gargants are easily avoided. The thunder of their footfalls makes it very easy to hear them coming, and their meaty, grasping hands are not dextrous enough to catch well-hidden prey. On the field of battle, however, there is no escape.

The appeal of full-scale battle for the gargant is understandable. Their daily existence is one fraught with hunger and pain; with the Age of Chaos having ravaged the lands and corrupted so much of their natural habitats, merely finding enough food to sustain themselves is an ongoing struggle. In times of war, however, there is always good eating to be had. Each corpse-field is a banquet laid out for whoever has the strength to claim it. Gargants are no mere scavengers, though; many will hunt out battle in the same manner that primitive peoples hunt prey-beasts. They make war not just to fill their extensive bellies, but because they love the thrill of it. No longer are they outsized monsters repeatedly lashed by the elements, challenged by would-be heroes and often starved to near exhaustion by their own ravenous metabolisms; on the day of battle, they are gods.

All gargants have learned to recognise the hundreds-strong footprints of an army on the march. They will follow these trails with long, determined strides, hoping to find a good scrap at the end. With the Mortal Realms under such constant threat from the hordes of anarchy and destruction, it is never long before they spot a battle in which to revel in their raw power. As the screams and crashing tumult of conflict reaches them on the wind, the gargant will break into a loping run, leaving deep footprints in the earth as he pounds across the wilderness. In the Heartlands of Ghur, those who hear the signature *thump-thump-thump* of a charging gargant will do everything in their power to find safe haven before the enormity crests the horizon and starts to lay about himself with his titanic club. Unfortunately, when a gargant is in full stride, even agility and swiftness is no defence. Should a gargant be irritated by a distant foe, he will scoop up a chunk of fallen masonry or even an enemy warrior and hurl it – though his aim is poor, any so much as clipped by such a devastating projectile will be broken and likely slain.

SIZE IS EVERYTHING

Many of the more brutish races of the realms believe that 'might makes right'. The majority of greenskin society, for instance, revolves around that simple concept. Though the gargants are not greenskins, or at least not by birth, they subscribe to the same tenets. Some even believe that 'mightier makes rightier', and whenever two really big gargants cross one another's path they will wrestle, brawl, roar and engage in contests of strength to show their dominance. Their preoccupation with size as an indication of prowess no doubt hails from their belief that the godbeast Behemat, the World Titan, was so eye-poppingly huge he was able to crush mountains with the flat of his hand. But even he was not the first of his kind. Gargant legend also features the grandfather of their race, known as Ymnog, who was only ever bested by Sigmar. Some say Ymnog was so tall his head scraped the stars, and that the God-King had to cheat to kill him, using storm magic instead of honest strength. The truth is lost in the mists of time. Behemat, Ymnog's son, is a much more immediate ancestor for the gargant race to revere. Until recently the World Titan was just sleeping off the effects of his own duel against Sigmar, slumbering beneath the Everspring Swathe. The attempts Archaon the Everchosen made to enslave Behemat during the Realmgate Wars, and the godbeast's subsequent mercy killing from the hammer Ghal Maraz, have changed gargant society forever.

THE GODSTOMPA

The gargant preoccupation with feet, and the acts of stomping and generally kicking things, is all interlinked with their perception of the deity Gorkamorka, who some tribes know as the Godstompa. Gargants see only things even bigger than they as worthy of their respect, and there are none larger than the two-headed god himself. The manifestation of Gorkamorka's great green foot, as called into being by the shamans of the greenskins,

has been witnessed many times by the gargants that fight alongside orruks, stamping up and down on enemy cavalry formations and even crushing dragons flat. To them, these manifestations of godly power are proof that Gorkamorka is truly immense, and therefore worthy of a rough sort of worship.

Some gargant tribes even believe that Gorkamorka is not humanoid at all, but rather a pair of immense, yellow-nailed feet – a Gorkfoot, which is stompy but kicky, and a Morkfoot, which is kicky but stompy. Ultimately, it is to Gorkamorka that Behemat and even Ymnog owed their allegiance. In the Age of Myth, Gorkamorka was effectively Behemat's leader, or 'big heel', and the World Titan fought as his champion. For many centuries they roamed together, blissfully smashing everything they came across, but as Chaos took hold on the realms, their friendship turned to a fierce rivalry, and rivalry into a violent demise.

THE INFECTIOUS WAAAGH!

The hordes of Destruction are known for gathering a deadly momentum. When this reaches critical levels, the greenskin hordes surge forwards, bellowing something called a 'Waaagh!'. The sheer energy of this phenomenon is contagious, and can even inflame the minds of those gargants who hear it. After all, with everyone bawling and stomping around them, the gargants are loath to be left out: bawling and stomping are very much their thing. All the noise and excitement has an intoxicating effect on the gargant race; though it does not set their blood alight with an unstoppable fervour as it does with the orruks, it does make them more aggressive and bellicose. The gargants get caught up in the furore and lumber alongside the greenskins, shouting at the tops of their voices and occasionally breaking into a run through sheer exuberant battlelust. A tribe of charging gargants can break an enemy battleline in moments, jumping up and down and squashing entire ranks of the foe until all cohesion is lost. Vast fortresses have their walls collapsed by charging Mega-Gargants that shoulder through ancient masonry and club down gun-studded watchtowers. These monstrosities are the hideous face of the destructive hordes that roam the realms – and when they all face the same direction with the same intent, the civilised races pay a terrible price.

A cannonball struck Oddro Sharkchewer right in the chest. Coughing painfully, Oddro glared up at the artillery emplacements atop the duardin dam. He felt wetness on his lips, wiping his mouth to find a red smear of blood. It reminded him of that time he smashed up the galleon with all the guns – there would be one hell of a bruise in the morning. 'Now ya done it, ya bleedin' shortlings,' he boomed. 'You're all going to die. Bash it down, lads!' Oddro waved his tribe forward, stamping along the riverbed in great spuming fountains of ice water.

More cannonballs hit home. One punched through his leg, ripping open an artery. Another smashed the galleon's prow he had strapped to his shoulder. A third ploughed into the lake at his knee. Oddro felt the stinging impacts of shooting-sticks as duardin gunners, nested in the eye sockets of the bearded faces grimacing from the dam's fascia, took their potshots.

Oddro tensed and leapt, clearing the remaining distance to the dam and bringing his shipwrecka club down to hammer the battlements flat. A web of cracks raced across the dam wall. Artillery crews – fancy cannons and all – toppled screaming to their deaths in the river below. Boshdo Blackhood hit the wall at full charge, nearly knocking himself out – the Gatebreaker had never been the brightest – but more of the dam wall cracked at the impact. Garrad War-dog, coming under attack from rotor-machines that whirred like insects around him, swatted and punched the duardin machines from the skies before kicking the dam hard. Oddro smashed his club into the same cratered section of the stonework over and over until water shot through in a dozen places. Then the dam burst, and a hundred bearded shortlings were carried away in the sudden tidal wave. Oddro grinned as water gushed around him. It was time for the feast to begin.

To fight the Sons of Behemat is to fight the titans of legend. The gargant race sees its enemies as vermin who exist only to be crushed, hurled and eaten. The killing blade causes them but a scratch, the well-aimed arrow is no more than a pinprick, the blazing spell scorches but does not slow. Only the most valiant or cunning stand a chance.

THE AGE OF MYTH

The history of the gargant race is not recorded in writing, but instead passed down as an oral history amongst the matriarchs of each tribe. From scraps of ancient legend about the Godstompa Gorkamorka and his champion, Behemat, the gargants learn not wisdom, nor caution, but ambition – and a taste for acts of truly mythic violence.

The storytelling tradition of the gargants includes several tales from the Age of Myth. Most of them begin with the rivalry between Gorkamorka and Behemat. After the greenskin god was freed by Sigmar from his entrapment inside the Living Avalanche, Drakatoa, his anarchic existence had a kind of focus, for he was charged with destroying the monsters that preyed on Sigmar's cities. The Realm of Beasts was soon strewn with the corpses of behemoths, some so large that entire tribes of barbarians made their homes within their skulls.

From deep in the Realm of Chaos, the Chaos Gods whispered into Gorkamorka's mind, saying the twin-headed deity was nothing more than a slave to Sigmar's will. Meanwhile, the godbeast Behemat still wandered as he pleased; untroubled by duty and with his head quite literally in the clouds, he killed, ate or snored away whole months at a time without a care in the world. Gorkamorka began to resent the fact that his champion roamed free whilst he took on an endless task at the behest of another. He split himself in twain so his Mork side could better think of a cunning solution. Gork's simple desire to bash things to death was undermined by Mork's suspicion he was being used. As the god reformed under the Bad Moon, a gleam of malice appeared in Gorkamorka's bloodshot eye.

From that point on, whenever Gorkamorka encountered Behemat, he would issue his champion a challenge that the father of gargants could not refuse. He was to replicate one of the twin-headed god's own feats of strength, or die in the attempt. The first of these tasks was to cause a great flood that destroyed a city. Once, after a year-long monster hunt that spanned the Desiccating Desert of Hysh, Gorkamorka had quenched his godly thirst by drinking so much of the Gleaming Bay that the sea level dropped. Then, when the ocean was sure the greenskin god was gone, it surged back to such a level it flooded the coastal city of Omnitopia. This 'great watering' was a feat that Gorkamorka urged Behemat to replicate. The father of gargants gladly took up the challenge. Soon enough he submerged a city – albeit unintentionally – by tripping over a fjord's wrinkly bits and belly-flopping in the Girdlesea near the aelven city of Araxia. The gold-walled metropolis was flooded by

the resulting tsunami, and Behemat gleefully helped himself to the priceless treasures that had become so much flotsam. Since then, the gargants say, a great many aelves have made their homes under the sea to escape similar catastrophes.

Not long afterward Gorkamorka slew an entire generation of gigadroths rampaging across the Great Parch, in doing so saving Sigmar's burgeoning civilisations from death by fire. Gorkamorka charged Behemat with a similar feat – to stop the supervolcano Vulcatrix's Lair from birthing hundreds more of the beasts. Behemat wrenched the top half of Mount Krolosid from its roots, turned it upside down, and shoved its peak roughly into the caldera of the Lair like a cork in a bottle. This caused a nation of

angry red-bearded duardin to rise up against Behemat, but as rivers of magma spurted and burned all around, he stomped the volcano-worshipping warriors flat. The duardin of the mountains have been born short and squat ever since.

Another tale speaks of the time Dracothion took his revenge upon Gorkamorka for knocking him unconscious after Sigmar freed the greenskin god from Drakatoa's amber prison. A rain of blazing meteors, sent from the heavens at great speed, struck Gorkamorka as he slept, but so tough was his skin it did no more than leave pockmarks and scabs across his body. Gorkamorka challenged Behemat to endure a similar barrage. His champion stood atop the highest mountain in Azyr, bellowing insults at Dracothion that ranged from the crude to the downright offensive. Sure enough, a barrage of celestial meteors hammered down. Behemat took a good few of them on the chin, but when the pain grew too great he thwacked the last one as hard as he could with his warclub, sending it back up to strike Dracothion himself. The Great Drake's scales fell down in a silvery meteor shower, and as they fell to earth, taking form as the saurian Seraphon so they could bite the gargant race forever more.

Taking a new tack in his rivalry, Gorkamorka challenged Behemat to a great eating competition. The contest started in Ghur, with Gorkamorka devouring all those monsters he had slain over the years – even those that had long rotted away, for his stomach knew no fear of the dead. Behemat ate fewer monsters than Gorkamorka, but then plunged through the Greedmouth Realmgate to Shyish. There he ate the gheists of those same monsters as well, in doing so cleaning his plate better than the greenskin god. The monster-gheists did not fill him up for long, so he ate his way through a nation of menfolk as well. Since then, the dead men of Shyish have had no meat on their bones at all.

RISE OF THE WORLD TITAN

The World Titan had proven himself the equal of a god – or so he thought. Having spawned a thousand young since the death of Ymnog, and having matched Gorkamorka deed for deed thus far in his trials, Behemat thought himself unstoppable. It was the God-King Sigmar and his own warriors that put the lie to his claim.

The last of Behemat's Feats was a fine challenge indeed. He was to fight the thunder god Sigmar to a standstill, something that Gorkamorka had achieved where Ymnog – Behemat's father – had failed. During the Great Storm of Verdia, Behemat armoured himself with the slab-like sides of the Nevergreen Peaks and bellowed a challenge to Sigmar so loud that the forests shivered in fear for miles around. The trees of the lands were so scared they still shiver to this day whenever a storm gathers. But only when the World Titan started grinding the mountain fastnesses of Sigmar's people under his heel did the God-King descend like a meteor from the firmament.

Sigmar and Behemat battled with such ferocity their blood fell in great torrents, forming the waterfalls of the mountains. At the last, Sigmar struck Behemat on the chin with Ghal Maraz, a blow that would have shattered mountains. Such was the godbeast's legendary constitution even that did not kill him. Behemat stumbled away, stunned and reeling, until he reached Harmonis Veldt. Still dazed, he gorged himself on the local fauna before vomiting up an entire generation of gargants, a last great feat of propagation before he finally allowed himself to collapse. The godbeast stumbled and fell like a tree, landing so hard he became embedded in Ghyran's crust.

Behemat lay unconscious for millennia. The lands formed over him, his lumpen immensity blending with the landscape. Travellers roamed his recumbent form without ever knowing that they walked the hide of a godbeast. So deep was his slumber that even the plague-spreading invasions of the Age of Chaos elicited no more than the occasional shudder. The people of the Sprawl put these down to earthquakes, though the gargants of that land – having long ago crawled from Behemat's maw – knew it was their forefather stirring. What they did not realise was that the infections of the land had been sent by Archaon as a deliberate act of war.

The Everchosen had long coveted Azyr, for it was the one realm that remained out of his reach. His plan was to enslave the godbeasts Ignax and Behemat, using their immense strength and power to break open the gates to the Realm of Heavens. To bring Behemat under his spell, Archaon intended to enchant the floating island known as the Great Green Torc, a horseshoe-shaped landmass that embodied the twelve seasons of Ghyran, and use it as a slave collar to control him. With the plagues of Nurgle ravaging the Torc, and the Scabrous Sprawl likewise infected, the World Titan would be rendered biddable and confused – at which point he would be unleashed upon the Gates of Azyr itself.

Divining that Archaon's plan threatened to capsize a vast swathe of Ghyran, and perhaps even Azyr beyond it, Sigmar sent his Stormcast Eternals to intervene. Their mission was to destroy the forces of Nurgle that infected the Scabrous Sprawl and the warpstone-addled skaven of the Clans Skryre that had been sent to drill down into the nerve centres of Behemat's recumbent form and thereby rouse him to wrath. It was the actions of Lord Gardus of the Hallowed Knights, working in concert with Thaddeon ven Denst of the Anvils of the Heldenhammer, that saw the Great Green Torc cleansed of taint. On the landscape beneath it, the Hammers of Sigmar fought alongside the Knights Excelsior to destroy the skaven and hence prevent Behemat from being awoken from his slumber.

They were too late. The warp drills of the skaven had roused Behemat to a state of demented agony, and he began to rise. Chasms and fissures split the land as he lifted his great right hand, mountains revealed as knucklebones and cities built atop his fingers toppling away. The land convulsed, causing tidal waves a continent away. On Tor Crania, a bloodshot eye the size of a small lake blinked open and stared madly at the stormy skies.

It was the goddess Alarielle that passed the death sentence upon the World Titan. From nearby Athelwyrd she had watched him sleep, but left him to his peace. In her melancholy she had chosen isolation rather than a last act of defiance as Nurgle's endless armies conquered Ghyran, and divined that the godbeast was now infected beyond recovery. That tragic message reached not only the Stormcast Eternals, but also Dracothion. The Great Drake sent his draconic children to war, the finest warriors in the Stormhosts riding atop them to charge hard into the Nurgle worshippers crawling like lice over the resurgent Behemat. But even the Extremis Chambers in their full glory could not save the raging titan.

It was the Great Bolts that slew Behemat, in the end, just as they had slain his father before him. Harnessed by the Celestant-Prime, they were delivered by the most powerful weapon in Sigmar's service: Ghal Maraz, that relic from another time that men called the Great Shatterer. The lightning-wreathed hammer blasted into the forehead of Behemat, succeeding where the fury of the Extremis Chambers had failed by killing him stone dead. Since that day the godbeast's remains have dominated the Scabrous Sprawl, part of his rotting ribcage forming an immense structure that is now used as a hall of commerce.

The death of Behemat led to a strange phenomenon amongst his sons and daughters. Haunted by strange echoes of his demise, the gargants have slowly been getting larger in size, with some of the most recent generations growing over a hundred feet tall. Amongst the eldest and most widely travelled gargants, it is said that there will one day be another World Titan – that one amongst them will become so large they will take up the role in the zodiacal order of the cosmos that Behemat left behind. Some of their number have begun to ape Behemat's mythical victories, whether consciously or otherwise – causing avalanches in mountainous regions, sweeping tidal waves into coastal cities, and stamping on fault lines to precipitate earthquakes. One day, a true contender for the title of World Titan will appear – and on that day the Mortal Realms will quake in fear.

YMNOG, GRANDFATHER OF GARGANTS

Ymnog was one of the first zodiacal godbeasts, and even thousands of years after their ancestor's death the gargants fear to rouse his ire. The First Titan had a temper so great he once broke reality itself with his club, shattering it into three fragments and thereby forming land, sea and sky. Afterwards, Ymnog swallowed the comets from the heavens and washed them down with a full half of the First Ocean. Sated, he lay down, his weight splitting the earth and creating the chasms of the realms. As he slept, his mouth agape, his drool formed the rivers of the land and his snore the thunder of the first storms. Whilst Ymnog slumbered, Behemat and his kin grew from the stones within his belly. Desperate to escape, Behemat brewed a lake of potent moonshine in the squelching marshland of his father's guts. It was so foul and so potent it made Ymnog retch up Behemat and his siblings into his mouth. Escape was close at hand. However, two of the gargants, Gorg and Ama-Gorag, had a mighty thirst, and had drunk deep of the liquor. As the two behemoths brawled over a jar of vomit upon Ymnog's tongue, the godbeast shut his great mouth with a thunderclap, swallowing the siblings back down forever. Only Behemat made it out alive. He hammered at Ymnog's teeth, but his sire would not open his yawning maw. From the broken splinters of Ymnog's fangs were created the first mountains.

LAND OF THE GARGANTS

Ghur, the Realm of Beasts, is reckoned to be the ancestral home of the gargant race. It is here Gorkamorka slew the greatest of monsters, here that Behemat's mighty deeds left their mark, both on the landscape and the culture of the savage tribes that roam across it. In these primeval, ever-hungry wastelands, only the strong survive.

It takes a very determined effort to stop a gargant from sitting down wherever he wants to. Some are so large that when asleep they are mistaken for features of the landscape. As a result, gargants can be found in every realm, making their homes in dank mountain caves, holed up in shattered temples and slumbering away in the clearings of deep forests. In shrouded Ulgu there are shadow-skinned gargants that trail mist behind them as they slip through the gloom; in High Azyr there are mason-giants in the employ of Sigmar; in glittering Chamon there are gargants clad head to foot in scrap metal or even wearing fitted armour earned as a reward for mercenary services. Yet these towering monstrosities are most common of all in Ghur, the Realm of Beasts. There the rugged and muscular outlook of the gargant finds an ecosystem within which it can truly thrive, for it is a world never short of red meat.

There is a simple rule that governs all of Ghur's lands, from the most primordial to those forcibly ground under the heel of Chaos rule – hunt, or be hunted. Even the rugged terrain obeys this fundamental principle. A traveller who spends a long night recovering from his exertions may awake the next day to see the land has changed around him, with the horizon slightly different from the evening before. Here, the mountains are alive, grinding across the savannah with slow but perceptible movements. The trees seek to drain all life from the earth with their hungering tendrils, driving the iron-hard tips of their roots into fallen beasts and sleeping travellers to suck out their sustenance. The rivers carve their way across the lands with a high-speed erosion, the rocks they chew from the hills and mountains of their birth acting as gnawing molars that gouge and bite amongst a constant tumult of white water.

Living glaciers hunger to freeze the rivers in turn, or to throttle inland seas with their ice-floe young. Even Ghur's tectonic plates hunt each day, grinding one atop another as they attempt to bury their rivals – a chalk mark made at the bottom of a cliff or plateau will be buried by day's end as the landmass's edge rumbles ever onwards. This phenomenon makes earthquakes a common occurrence in Ghur; no few cities of order have been tumbled as a result of failing to account for the shifting, bad-tempered movements of the landscape. The volatility of the realm is interpreted in many ways by their denizens. The gargants consider Ymnog to have shaped the lakes and gulches with his footprints, whereas the ogor mawtribes see each chasm in the landscape as a great devouring maw put there by the Gulping God, and the grots see each fissure as the claw-marks of Boingob, the godbeast squig. Perhaps all of them are right, and perhaps none at all.

The effect a tribe of gargants can have upon the environment is profound. They leave their mark everywhere they walk – not just in the case of their massive, spatulate footprints, but in the trail of devastation they leave behind them. A gargant will push over a grave-cairn, rip down a sacred tree's branches, or step on a candleshrine simply to pass the time as he hunts for his next meal or lumbers in search of pastures new.

Should a gargant reach a Ghurish frontier town or a makeshift keep some optimistic settlers have built to defend a place of importance, he will kick down the walls, punch over the spires and knee the brickwork into ruin just to see the denizens run screaming for their lives. This makes gargants a natural enemy for those few brave souls who have taken it upon themselves to bring civilisation to the Realm of Beasts. Because the trail of a gargant can be seen by the scattering of mangled, half-eaten corpses and smoking buildings he leaves behind him, the life of a would-be gargant slayer is simple when it comes to hunting down their targets – right up until the point they actually find them.

The exception to this rule is the Kraken-eater, that subculture of Mega-Gargant that tends to prowl the coastlines. Wading waist deep or even up to the neck in the oceanic waters, they leave scant trail indeed, so much so that only the Idoneth Deepkin have the knack of tracking them. The shattered wreckage of the ships and galleons they prey upon is little help in discerning their whereabouts, for it floats upon the waves, dispersed by the tides to wash up on the serrated, teeth-like rocks of the Ghurish coasts.

Those hunter-scavengers who seek to salvage sodden treasures from the detritus of such vessels will find themselves coming up empty handed; the Kraken-eater will already have taken all the good stuff for himself. The cunning few who take the role of wreckers are in for an even nastier surprise. Their false lights, intended to lure unwary ships to founder on the biting rocks of the coasts just as an angler-shark lures in its prey, may instead attract a Mega-Gargant that launches itself up from the water, climbs atop the cliff in one smooth motion, and shovels them into its stinking maw before they can recover from the shock.

FANGATHRAK, THE MAWGATE

The All-gate of Ghur is not static, as with the other giant portals that lead to the Eightpoints. Instead it is held inside the gaping, cavernous mouth of the godbeast Fangathrak, the world-worm, a beast so large its trail of devastation leaves valleys in its wake. Once, this impossible monstrosity was bound by the Crawlerforts, vast crab-like beasts with Chaos Dreadholds upon their backs. Each fort had a godly chain that helped bind Fangathrak in place. At the end of the Realmgate Wars, however, the orruk warlord Gordrakk initiated a three-way battle between his warclans, the Stormcast Eternals and the Chaos worshippers that sought to control the Mawgate-beast. Enraged by the Waaagh! energy, the world-worm Fangathrak broke its bonds and burrowed swiftly to escape the Crawlerforts. It was last seen in the Ghurish Heartlands, heading south.

STOMPING GROUNDS

The Heartlands of Ghur constantly war with themselves, one continent devouring another as the seas claw and writhe to take on new coastlines. In the last few centuries, the mesa-studded land of Donse has been crushed between Thondia in the north and Andtor to the south, with the two rival landmasses competing to take its rocky carcass for themselves. In the west, Rondhol closes its coastal jaws on those of Gallet, even as the frost-locked land of Bjarl inveigles fjords into its underside and chokes Andtor's southern coast with ice floes. If a scholar was to somehow map the Heartlands, he would find his document hopelessly out of date within a matter of decades.

The Heartlands are situated perhaps two weeks' travel southward from Ghur's innermost point, and are host to several tribes of gargants. Since the Age of Sigmar, humans have begun to settle the region. Excelsis and Izalend, built on the Coast of Tusks, have grown large indeed on that relatively stable region, for their chose continent Thondia is an alpha predator amongst its kin, and unlikely to be devoured. Even the Ossiarch Empire has put forth its claim, building a citadel of bone near the Krakensea that has yet to fall.

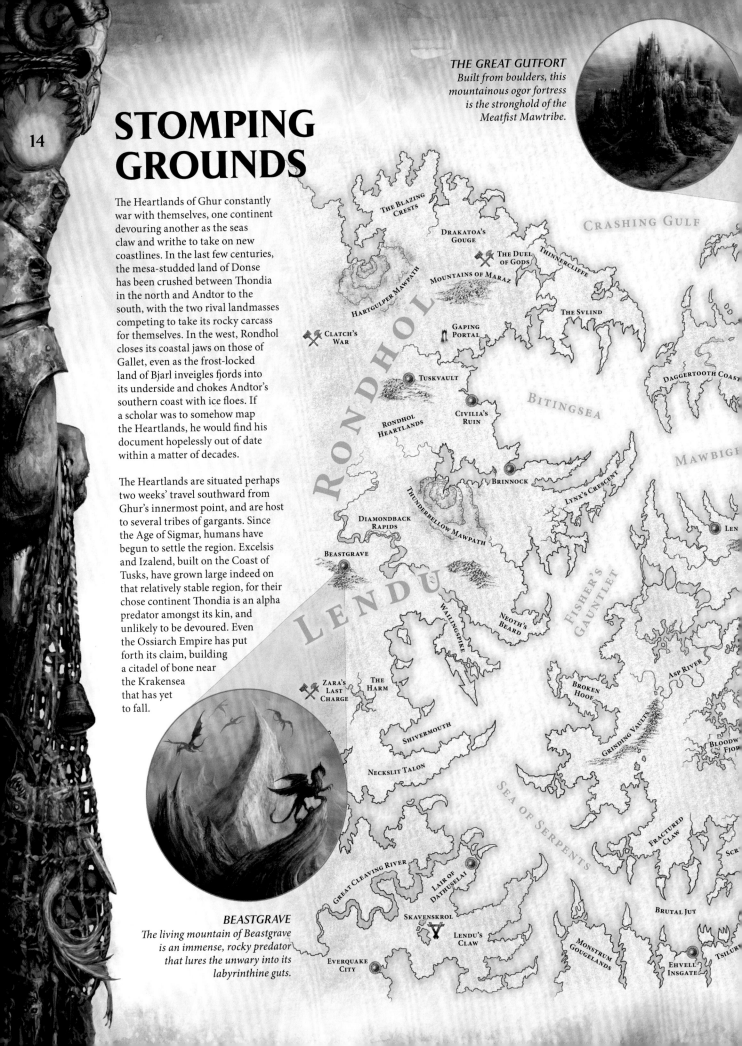

THE GREAT GUTFORT
Built from boulders, this mountainous ogor fortress is the stronghold of the Meatfist Mawtribe.

BEASTGRAVE
The living mountain of Beastgrave is an immense, rocky predator that lures the unwary into its labyrinthine guts.

CRASHING GULF

THE BLAZING CRESTS

DRAKATOA'S GOUGE

THE DUEL OF GODS

THINNERCLIFFE

HARTGULPER MAWPATH

MOUNTAINS OF MARAZ

THE SVLIND

CLATCH'S WAR

GAPING PORTAL

DAGGERTOOTH COAST

RONDHOL

TUSKVAULT

BITINGSEA

RONDHOL HEARTLANDS

CIVILIA'S RUIN

MAWBIGH

BRINNOCK

LYNX'S CRESCENT

THUNDERBELLOW MAWPATH

LEN

DIAMONDBACK RAPIDS

BEASTGRAVE

LENDU

FISHER'S GAUNTLET

NEOTH'S BEARD

WAILINGSPIKE

ASP RIVER

BROKEN HOOF

ZARA'S LAST CHARGE

THE HARM

SHIVERMOUTH

GRINDING VAULTS

BLOODW FJOR

NECKSLIT TALON

FRACTURED CLAW

SCR

SEA OF SERPENTS

GREAT CLEAVING RIVER

LAIR OF DATHUSLAI

BRUTAL JUT

SKAVENSKROL

LENDU'S CLAW

MONSTRUM GOUGELANDS

EVERQUAKE CITY

EHVELL'S INSGATE

TSILUR

GHURISH HEARTLANDS

EXCELSIS
A city built around the titanic Spear of Mallus, Excelsis mines prophetic 'glimmerings'.

15

MANGREL ISLE
THE RAVENIDS
THE DRENCH
THUNDERSCORN PEAKS
IZALEND
ICEFANGS
CLAWING SEA
VENSOTH BAY
THE GREAT GUTFORT
GREAT EXCELSIS ROAD
COAST OF TUSKS
THE STAMPING
MEATFIST MAWPATH
KRONDSPINE RANGE
BILGEPORT
THE MAR
LAKE EVERGLUT
THONDIA
URSRICHT'S KILL
GLOSSOM CREVASSE
EXCELSIS
SPEAR OF MALLUS
THE GNARLWOOD
VEXOTHSKOL
KRONDSKOL
BREAKFACE MAWPATH
MORRUK HILLS
QUESTING SERPENT RIVER
FRAKTOA CREVASSE
STONE NAUTILOR
LOST MESAS
BLOODGULLET MAWPATH
YMNOG'S TRAMPLE (NORTH)
NAUTIL PEAKS
CARCASS DONSE
TEMPLIA BEASTHALL
GALLET
RIVER SLANNSTONGUE
KOATL'S GULLET
PRIMEVAL JUNGLE
CRAWLING PITS OF GHARRENTIA
MEKITOPSAR
OLDBRAWL MAWPATH
UNDERCHASM GULCH
PLAINS OF MEKITOPSAR
BROKENJARL MAWPATH
GREATPEAKS OF ANDTOR
GODSWALLOW DELTA
LAKE HOARFROST
RAVENING RIVERS
MOULDERPIT
NECK A
FASTING VELDT
ANDTOR
BANTU'S GATE
THE GNAWING FORDS
RIMELAKE
EVERWINTER'S CLAIM
ICEBROW
BJARL THROAT
KRAKENSEA
SHATTERLAND FLOES
HARASSIC CLIFFS
GREEDMOUTH
RAMHUT'S SPINE
COLOSSAL BITE
LOOKAWAY POINT
YMNOG'S TRAMPLE (SOUTH)
BJARL
CORPSE LAKES
RUINS OF VENTIVIA
DEFFGORGE
WAR OF BASILISKS
FANGSGIRDLE
WAKE OF FANGATHRAK
DRAKBITER MAWPATH
LAKE MAW
THE IVORY CITADEL
R-LUPARL'S SHELLPEAKS
GHURISH NECROSIA

WHEN ROUSED TO WRATH

The death of Behemat sent shockwaves through gargant society. Twinned with the coming of the Nighthaunts – a foe that the gargants could not simply crush underfoot – the events of the Age of Sigmar had a profound effect on the race's psyche. But in a mind as simple as that of a gargant, fear and uncertainty can soon lead to rage.

The Age of Myth was an epoch of glory for the gargants. After all, in a time when the lands themselves were shaped by those with the might to make it so, they had a natural advantage. The Age of Chaos saw that supremacy turned upon its head. With the warbands devoted to the Dark Gods rampaging across the lands and scores of would-be conquerors seeking ways to prove their might, even the largest gargants were hunted by warlords eager for such a prestige kill. With the ferocity and ingenuity of the human mind twinned with the gifts of their daemonic patrons, it soon became clear that this new breed posed a real danger. Some used disease and plague as a weapon, poisoning the gargants before closing in for the kill. Others used illusion, attacking the mind rather than the body. Some even came amidst a howling tumult of daemonic energy so intense the gargants found themselves staying well away, or even joining the ranks of Chaos to ensure their survival.

The Age of Sigmar brought a new era of war to gargant kind. Many who had pledged their allegiance to the Dark Gods found themselves assailed by gleaming paladins and resplendent riders atop celestial Stardrakes, and were hunted once more. Likewise, those gargants who meted out destruction upon the innocent and the impoverished, seeking easy pickings, were attacked by Sigmar's new armies. Even then, the new force in the realms were opponents the gargants could understand – and crush beneath their feet, even if they had the bad manners to discorporate in a flash of energy rather than leaving a juicy corpse behind. It was the grand work of Nagash, however, that was to shake the gargant race to its core.

At first, the events of Time of Tribulations affected the gargants to a lesser extent than perhaps any other race in the Mortal Realms.

They paid little mind to omens such as dead crows falling by the hundred from the skies or strange patterns of bones appearing on the mountainsides; such things they considered literally beneath their notice. Even the Shyish necroquake was dismissed, at first, as a freak occurrence that had little to do with them – though their greenskin allies, who called the howling, shrieking wave of Shyishan energy that capsized the realms the 'Deffstorm', seemed uncharacteristically tense about the matter.

The Arcanum Optimar that followed saw all of the realms beset by strange manifestations of magic as shamans and sorcerers set loose ever more powerful spells. In Ghur, the godbeast Ravenak writhed and howled in its prison, spectral echoes of its gnashing fangs chomping anything it could get its teeth into – including those gargants too curious or stupid to get out of the way. The mercenary gargant Dolf the Black, upon seeing a Purple Sun of Shyish floating eerily past him in the Vale of Broken Skulls, ran up to the predator-spell and gave it a good kick – only to find his leg turning to amethyst crystal. Those gargants who sought to use drifting Penumbral Pendulums as large and impressive weapons often lost a hand or two for their trouble, or were even cut in half. But overall, the gargants saw the wild spells roaming the lands more as distractions or curios rather than true dangers.

It was the coming of the Nighthaunt processions that heralded the greatest change in the gargants' mindset. At first the brutish race merely watched, dumbfounded, as swathes of gheists drifted past them to work the vengeance of Nagash. Where the gargants came into direct conflict they would stamp and crush the Nighthaunts just as they would any other foe. Only one who strikes a Nighthaunt with courage and self-belief has the wherewithal to kill it, for the coward's blade will simply pass straight through, but the sheer force of the gargants' conviction gave them the edge they needed.

The Mortarch of Grief, Lady Olynder, was the first to teach the gargants the true meaning of fear. As she passed through the Greatpeaks of Andtor on her way to treat with the Ossiarchs of the Ivory Host, her Nighthaunts were attacked by the native gargants that were massing there under the monstrous gargant warlord Lorge Skybiter. Lorge made haste to attack the leader of the enemy force, for she appeared to him no more than a wisp. As they duelled atop the edge of the gulch it soon became clear he had underestimated his foe. A single touch from the Mortarch's delicate, bony hand turned Lorge into nothing more than scattering of black roses that tumbled away on screaming winds.

Lorge's demise was witnessed by dozens of gargants, and the seed of uncertainty took hold. At Olynder's command, two of the warlord's lieutenants were hacked apart by the spectral wraiths that whirled around them, their flesh flensed from their bones even as they broke and ran. Banshees howled and shrieked around the heads of lesser gargants, turning their minds to mush as they swatted and tore at trails of ectoplasm to no effect. As Olynder's macabre spells turned the seeping, crawling sensation of fear that was spreading amongst the gargants into a primal terror, the raw confidence of the gargants faded to nothing. Even those giants stamping down on the Chainrasp hordes found their feet passing harmlessly through their adversaries. The resultant confusion turned slowly to panic, and over a long and bloody day of battle, most of the giants were cut down. Olynder deliberately let three of the gargants escape, her ethereal riders chasing but never catching them so they would carry the news of the massacre to the Heartland tribes.

Haunted and unable to settle, the survivors of the Greatpeaks Massacre told dark tales of spectres that simply could not be stomped. The terror in their voices had more of an effect on the listeners than the stories themselves. The tales spread like a virus, carried by mercenary gargants and ogors that travelled far and wide, even taking the story through Realmgates to other realms. They were only reinforced wherever similar battles took place, becoming a self-fulfilling prophecy. Over the years, the gargant race learned that it was not a good idea to fight gheists, and that even the most vigorous stamping would have no effect. The indomitable soul of the gargant race quailed for the first time.

Salvation came from a strange source indeed. When the Bjarl Stomp made common cause with the Drakkfoot tribe of Bonesplitterz against a procession of bloodgheists crossing the Asp River, the gargants watched in awe as the savage orruks hacked the ectoplasmic host apart and dispelled their hexes by the simple expedient of shouting really loudly. The energy of the Waaagh! fanned the fires of the Bjarl Stomp's simmering anger, and they suddenly found themselves able to crush the gheists with ease. Their leader took on the name Ghost Stamper, swiftly rising to fame amongst the tribes. So began a strange war of self-belief as the tales of Asp River inspired as many gargant stomps as the Greatpeaks Massacre dampened. The resultant confusion turned to anger, which the Drakkfoot tribe stoked to incendiary levels. A new war against the dead had begun – one to prove the gargant race's might once and for all.

SIEGE OF THE TUSKVAULT

As the mayhem of the Arcanum Optimar took hold of the Mortal Realms, Sigmar's long-concealed Stormvaults were exposed – and the treasures within came within the reach of those brave or foolhardy enough to claim them. In the Rondhol region of the Ghurish Heartlands, Skragrott the Loonking gathered a grand horde of destruction so vast that Gordrakk, the Fist of Gork, agreed to lead it. A gargant stomp, led by Broguph Murgg with his siblings Slorgo and Mangor as his lieutenants, formed the vanguard of the force. The target of their attack was the Tuskvault in the Rondhol Scarland, for Skragrott had divined that this mountainous stronghold contained the Basha Shard, a fragment of Gorkamorka's own club that had splintered free in his duel with Sigmar. Legend had it that any who wielded the splinter-club could channel the greenskin god's immense strength, and though Skragrott himself was way too tiny to do so, a Mega-Gargant under his spell would be a formidable ally indeed. As the Bad Moon rose high, just as he had foreseen, the Loonking called a rain of jagged, tooth-like meteors to smash into the Tuskvault and destroy its protective mechanisms and force the gate ajar.

The Stormvault was far from undefended. The forests on the mountainside shivered as a force of Sylvaneth came to its defence, a brotherhood of Sigmar's chosen moving in support. Touramos, Lord-Arcanum of the Hammers of Sigmar, led several chambers of his kin from stormy skies to prevent Skragrott's alliance from gaining entrance to the vault. Bolstered by their own allies in the form of Fyreslayers of the Vostarg lodge, the Stormcast Eternals hurled back the metal-clad orruks that Gordrakk led into the fight even as a horde of Spiderfang grots ambushed the Sylvaneth in turn. Touramos' celestial magic seriously injured Broguph, violently electrocuting the gargant even as he attempted to shove the Lord-Arcanum into his fisher-net. Broguph was forced to lumber to safe ground.

Slorgo Murgg waded through the battle, scowling as Judicator arrows jutted from his skin. He seemed unstoppable until a mounted charge from the Extremis Chamber, led by Sargassus Heavenhost and the Celestant-Prime himself, bowled him over with the meteoric force of their assault. Mangor, however, made it to the gates of the Tuskvault. After bashing them over and over with a boulder the size of an outhouse, he began to prise them even further open, the squeal of grinding clockwork and tortured hydraulics cutting over the din of battle.

It was enough. Though Mangor was forced to fall back, batting away the Fyreslayers that hacked at his ankles, Skragrott and a swarm of robed Moonclan grots scurried away from the host of Prosecutors raining fire upon them and made it inside the Tuskvault. Moments later, the Stormcast Eternals and duardin were beset by Gordrakk's headlong assault. For a horrible moment, it seemed as if Skragrott's thieving grots would secure their prize. Then the Fyreslayer lords called up their most potent invocations, shaping the magma of the earth to burrow through the mountainous roof of the Stormvault. Bael-Grimnir shouted of his plan to Touramos, and the mage took to the skies upon his winged steed, blasting lightning at Mangor even as he defended the gate. Angered beyond reason, the Mega-Gargant climbed the mountainside in pursuit. With the immense weight of Mangor pushing down on the Tuskvault's magma-weakened roof, it gave way. The mountainside collapsed, burying the Stormvault under thousands of tons of rubble. Though Skragrott has resurfaced since that time, and though Mangor and the Brothers Murgg have largely recovered, the Basha Shard has been sealed away once more. Only time will tell if it will ever be unearthed.

THE STAMP OF HISTORY

The race of gargants has left a big impression on the history of the Mortal Realms. Though never quite organised enough to conquer nations, they have smashed countless cities and armies to ruin, in doing so changing the course of fate in a thousand ways. Only now are the denizens of the realms realising how much of a threat they truly pose.

● AGE OF MYTH ●

GLORIOUS DESTRUCTION

During the early days of the Age of Myth, Gorkamorka spends many a happy year beating to death anything that gets on his bad side, and generally revelling in his role as a god of brutal strength and low cunning. The godbeast Behemat is his right hand (or perhaps right foot), stamping flat many of the realm's deadliest creatures and smashing many a newly built city to dust. The first gargants crawl from Behemat's maw as he is sleeping, just as he crawled from that of his father Ymnog. They roam far and wide to batter the lands around them into submission.

ATTACK OF THE LIVING AVALANCHE

Gorkamorka meets his match in the form of Drakatoa. This godbeast is like no other; rather than being a monster that can be bashed over the head with a sufficiently large club, it is a mountainous mass of primordial amber with a malign sentience that sees it suffocate, entrap and digest everything it comes across – as the city of Bayrazine finds to its cost. Seeking a challenge, Gorkamorka takes his club to the creature, but cannot not deliver a killing blow, for Drakatoa had nothing in the way of bones to break or organs to rupture. Before he realises his mistake the twin-headed god is stuck fast in the sticky, gooey mess of his adversary's body, and soon submerged altogether. Nothing so mundane as suffocation or even digestion can lay low a god, but trapped as he is, Gorkamorka cannot escape. He spends many moons languishing within the Living Avalanche's guts, his anger burning hotter all the time.

AID FROM THE HEAVENS

It is Sigmar Heldenhammer that frees Gorkamorka. Seeing the greenskin god trapped within the amber mountain, he dives down from the heavens astride Dracothion the Great Drake and, using Ghal Maraz, smites the formless godbeast. As Sigmar lays about himself, Drakatoa is wracked with the energies of the storm. The Living Avalanche spits out Gorkamorka, still covered in thick amber goo. Instead of thanking the god that had freed him, however, Gorkamorka instantly goes on the attack; his rage is blinding, and he cares not where he vents it. His first act is to bring his club down upon Dracothion's head, knocking him unconscious with a single blow. Thereafter, the constellation of Dracothion has a nebula-scar across its brow, and the Great Drake a worsened temper to go with it.

Sigmar is incensed. He attacks Gorkamorka without hesitation, in doing so beginning a fight that lasts for many days and nights. The colossal impacts of Gorkamorka's club forms the chasms and valleys of the heartlands, those of Ghal Maraz the canyons and plateaus. Even the monstrous beasts of Ghur stop in their rampages to gawp at the destruction the two deities mete out upon each other. The two come to an understanding on the twelfth day, for they are warrior gods both, and strength has always respected strength. So is born an alliance between Gorkamorka and Sigmar, with the former agreeing to join the pantheon of the latter in exchange for uncontested hunting rights to the Realm of Beasts. In return, the God-King charges the orruk deity with ridding not just Ghur, but all the realms, of the most lethal monsters that haunt them. It was a task much to the twin-headed god's liking.

THE DEEDS OF BEHEMAT

Gorkamorka's gleeful rampage sours when the Chaos Gods convince him he is doing the bidding of Sigmar rather than acting of his own volition. He sees Behemat going about his business without a care, eating his fill and getting larger with every passing winter, and resolves to set the godbeast a series of tasks. Behemat somehow manages to succeed every one, sometimes even on purpose. Then, Gorkamorka challenges him to fight Sigmar. It does not end well, and Behemat is smote by Ghal Maraz, staggering away to disgorge hundreds of lesser gargants across Verdia before finally falling into a comatose state that lasts for hundreds of years. Gorkamorka takes some brief satisfaction in the fact before realising he is now bereft of his strongest and most trustworthy ally.

● AGE OF CHAOS ●

THE SPRAWL INFECTED

Nurgle, the Plague God, becomes besotted with the wondrous fecundity of Ghyran, and resolves to make it his. As part of his conquest of the Everspring Swathe, the area where Behemat lies – known as the Scabrous Sprawl – is riddled with plague. After long years of fighting with everything she has, Alarielle reaches the winter of her melancholy and retreats to her hidden haven, Athelwyrd. For centuries, Nurgle's power waxes. Behemat slumbers on, his sheer immensity protecting him against plagues so virulent they would have slain lesser beings a dozen times over.

THE PEAKS OF NARATOSIS

To the west of the Shyish Innerlands, the vaguely humanoid mountains known as the Nine Brothers are worshipped as demigods by the trapper-tribes of the Pho Tan foothills. The bone-wearing elders of the tribes insist the peaks were once gargants, frozen in place by the cold anger of Nagash when they tried to grind his skeletal worker-legions to bonemeal. However, with the rise of the nearby city Naratosis, such tales dwindle into legend. The recruiters that bribe the latest generation of Pho Tan youth into their services with powerful and impressive blackpowder weapons scoff at what they see is a primitive superstition, and soon the young men and women of Pho Tan speak no more of their ancestral tales to their comrades.

At the height of summer comes the Helltide, a conglomeration of Chaos-worshipping hosts so numerous even the Thousand Rifles cannot hold it back. The horde sacks Naratosis within a week, armour-clad knights of Chaos making free with the bounty of the city even as they bleed from shot-wounds that would have felled lesser warriors. From afar, the elders of the Pho Tan foothills see the city ablaze, and fear for their sons and daughters. They implore their mountain demigods for aid, travelling deep into yawning caves that look much like mouths and enacting rituals of supplication in the lightless caverns. It takes a full week, but their request is granted – at the expense of their lives. Only Danatura, the eldest of the clan, survives the journey into the peaks, for he was too infirm to go deep into the caves. Riding atop the shoulder of the largest of the Nine Brothers, he leads a second sack of Naratosis – but this time it is the forces of Chaos that are massacred. By week's end, the city and its invaders are no more. The Nine Brothers wander off towards the realm's centre in search of Nagashizzar – and a revenge millennia overdue.

THE SAVIOUR OF GLOSHEIM

After a season of being attacked by howling cannibals from the Skullsocket Hills, the traumatised people of Glosheim are visited by Elog Dampcloth, a wandering gargant in search of food and drink. The townsfolk give him the most part of that year's harvest to convince him to stay. For a time, Elog is happy enough getting drunk on Glosheim mead and breaking wind through people's windows. When the cannibals attack from the hills, Elog joins the people of the township in Glosheim's defence. He proves a critical asset. Glosheim's villagers fight with everything they have, and the bloodthirsty cannibals are driven off. Unfortunately, Elog gets carried away and runs after them, disappearing into the hills. Eight days later the gargant is back, painted head to foot in the skull-like rune of the Blood God. Glosheim's burgomeister screams in protest as he is caught up and eaten; without their prize asset, the townspeople are no match for the cannibal horde. Elog takes his promised share of the spoils – a full half of the corpses resultant from the battles thus far – and the surviving cannibals eat the rest. Within a month, Glosheim is a smoking ruin emptied of all life.

THE ARMOURED GARGANTS

Chaos-worshipping duardin raise the fire-belching, metal-limbed fortress rig of Zharr Vyxa in the waters of the Shyish Innerlands. Using their infernal industry they siphon the energies of the dead from Aquaenos, an underworld beneath the waters where a lost civilisation of ancient seafarers believed they would dwell in peace upon their death. As their underworld is drained of its magic the emissaries of Aquaenos emerge from the waters to broker a deal with nearby Athanasia, hoping for aid enough to sack Zharr Vyxa. With the riches of dead seafarer kings as collateral they enlist help from a dozen coastal villages around Hellspoint, and four Kraken-eater Mega-Gargants that agree to swim out to Zharr Vyxa and pull it apart. Unfortunately for the alliance, the Chaos duardin have gargants of their own, ensorcelled and clad in blackiron plate. So begins a fierce oceanic siege where the Mega-Gargants scale the fortress only to find themselves fighting against armoured Mancrushers backed up by hundreds of duardin artillerymen. Eventually the alliance is beaten back into the sea, and the underworld of Aquaenos drained completely of its magic until it is nothing more than undersea ruins. So much blood and ichor is spilled over the defence of Zharr Vyxa that the foaming waves of the Sea of Drowned Sorrows are stained red.

DONSE'S REVENGE

When a nomadic tribe of Chaos Marauders passes along the lip of the cliffs overlooking Donse, the ten elder gargants of that region climb out of the stricken land to lumber after their prey. In doing so they bite off more than they can chew, for when they close in on the Chaos worshippers they find them engaged in a daemon-summoning ritual that reaches its culmination mere minutes before the gargants make their attack. After a fierce battle against the bloodthirsty greater daemons that emerge from the ritual circle, the Donsian elders are slain. Not long after that, a great flood of gore fills the shallow basin at the once-arid heart of Carcass Donse, giving rise to a great deal of strange flora and fauna in the following years. Eating well as a result of the sudden natural bounty, a clutch of young gargants reaches massive proportions amongst the mesas and buttes. After many years of having their rule unchallenged, the young gargants resolve to leave Carcass Donse in search of battle, but to carry the memory of the land with them. On their discovery of ten massive gargant skeletons, each headless and with its bones etched with Chaos runes, the Donsers make a pact with one another that they will fight to destroy the legions of the Blood God or die in the attempt.

● AGE OF SIGMAR ●

THE REIGN OF KING BRODD

In Ghyran, the generation of gargants that crawled from Behemat's maw before his long slumber rules over the sky kingdom of the Great Green Torc. Born with intelligence and even a sense of basic morality, they rise above the scavenging ways of their race, learning the arts of the forge and making artefacts ranging from articulated plate armour to vast cannons capable of firing boulder-sized shot at any who dare assault their strongholds. Over centuries of isolation and deprivation brought on by the Age of Chaos, however, the Sky Titans begin to recede into atavism. They abandon the Great Green Torc to the Spiderfang grots and beastman tribes that infest it, hiding in the acrid reaches of the Sweatswamp to escape the plagues of Nurgle that ravage the land. There they remain for centuries. Only at the dawn of the Age of Sigmar do they emerge from seclusion, the rule of the gargant King Brodd galvanising them to join the fight against Archaon's hordes.

TO SCALE THE FLAMESPIRES

A gang of Aqshian Gatebreakers known as the Firehood Brothers scale the mist-shrouded heights of the Flamespires, those mountains in the Great Parch that house the city of Tempest's Eye. They are soon spotted by the airborne patrols of that region, closely monitored by gyrocopters and even Kharadron Frigates that keep within cannon range. The gargants lob rocks at the approaching craft, and the duardin are forced to withdraw to the middle distance, for the throwing arm of the gargant leader, Dankeg Moat-drinker, has been honed over centuries of boulder-hurling contests. Given that the Firehoods seem to be climbing the wrong mountain, however, they are simply kept at a distance until several Kharadron Ironclads return from a trading mission. It is only when the Ironclads come down from the clouds to engage the Firehood Brothers, who by this point have reached the tip of the adjacent peak, that the gargant plan becomes clear.

As a wing of Ironclads comes in to level a broadside, Dankeg's lads make a death-defying leap towards them. The first misses the jump by a fraction and plummets to his death, but Dankeg and Bronk grab the gunnels of the very Ironclads that are opening fire upon them. Using the Kharadron ships for purchase they swing and jump across the dizzying chasm between the mountains, landing with such force on the shoulders of the peak opposite they cause a massive avalanche even as the out-of-control duardin skyvessels crash hard in a series of fiery explosions. The Tempest Lords garrison fights hard to save their city from being torn apart by the remaining two Firehood Brothers. Though the Gatebreakers are eventually slain by Prosecutor reinforcements, they lay waste to almost a third of the mountain city.

THE FALL OF BEHEMAT

In the Everspring Swathe, Behemat is awoken by skaven parasite-engines. He rises, his mind aflame with anger and pain, only to be put down once and for all by the Celestant-Prime wielding an empowered Ghal Maraz.

THE BATTLE OF DEFFGORGE

During the war for the Mawgate, the Megaboss Dakkbad Grotkicker enlists the help of the gargants of Deffgorge. The chasm is a scar across the Heartlands of Ghur which is said to have been gouged by Gorkamorka's yellowed toenail, and few who stray inside ever emerge. After Dakkbad lures the Stormcasts into their chasm, the gargants wade into the greater fight between Gordrakk, the Stormcast Eternals, and the Chaos forces sent by Archaon that seek to claim the All-gate of Ghur. During the ensuing battle, the godbeast Fangathrak breaks its chains and burrows into the crust of the Realm of Beasts, leaving a miles-wide pit behind it that not even the Deffgorge gargants dare to enter. Years later Fangathrak surfaces in the south of the Heartlands, leaving a trail of devastation so impressive even mountains are smashed to ruin.

THE HEADS OF ARBALESTER

The mystery of the Stone Heads of Arbalester, considered one of the Wonders of the Realms, is finally solved as the necroquake breaks across Arbalester Island. The curse of petrification that created them – the legacy of Archmage Teclis and the mountain-dwelling aelf seers that buried the unfortunate gargants neck-deep with their spells of entombment – is finally broken. The enormous rocky heads turn back to flesh, roaring and bellowing in anger at the Bonesplitter orruks making camp around them. Over three months of hard digging, the chanting orruk tribes dig out the buried Mega-Gargants. It costs them as many as fifty boars a week to keep the gargants alive, and the bellowed invective from the immense gargants is consistent and obscene enough to offend even the orruks. Yet the Wurgogg Prophets insist the once-stone gargants are Gorkamorka's children come to life. They keep the faith, and the towering gargants of Arbalester are freed.

With a tribe of war-painted behemoths bent on carnage at the heart of their clan, the greenskins' next Waaagh! proves unstoppable. Dozens of stone outcrops are carved in the likenesses of the Arbalester gargants, many of which are brought to life by the shamans' spells. They take over not only the human-settled Northtail Island but also an entire archipelago of underworlds to the east of the Ossiarch Empire.

WAR IN THE DEPTHS

The Kraken-eaters of the Harassic Cliffs, sick to the hind teeth of Idoneth raiders attempting to kill them, join forces. They know the aelves are raiding from a nearby enclave, for after each attempt on their lives, the aelves make their hit-and-run retreats back to the same region of the ocean, thinking themselves safe once more purely by dint of the fact their metropolis is sited on the sea bed. Yet they have reckoned without two things – the bitter temperament of the Harassic giants, and their cavernous lung capacity. In the middle of the night, the gargants swim out to the last known locale of the Idoneth raiders. Grabbing handfuls of glowing jellyfish by the tentacles as a source of illumination, they take in the deepest breaths they can and dive down into the deeps. It is the sea that defeats them. As the light fades to pitch-black and the leagues go by, the gargants peel off one by one, out of breath and clawing for the surface.

Japeth Cannon-chucker and his old friend Donk the Rigga refuse to give up. They return to their lair, recovering a Kharadron skyvessel from their trophy cave, and swim back out, hauling the vessel's intact hull behind them. By turning the duardin-made hull upside down and trapping air beneath it, they form enough of a reservoir of air to make a dive down to the sea bed. There the Idoneth enclave of Dara'maedh shimmers in its own bubble of magical energy. Japeth and Donk waste no time in kicking over the beautiful minarets and squeezing to death the Allopexes that swim to stop them. As luck would have it the enclave's Akhelians are on a raid, and only a garrison force remains to defend it. The carnage the gargants wreak on the Idoneth's spired settlements and the chorrileum at its heart is impressive; though they are eventually forced to flee to the surface by a concerted Isharann attack, they do enough damage that the Idoneth raids on the Kraken-eaters' coastal lairs cease altogether.

THE SPIDER KING
After imbibing too much 'nasty moonshine' given to him by the malicious grot Brewgits of Gharrentia, the gargant Greedy Hekk stumbles into the spider-haunted Crawling Pits. His fall is arrested by the ropey cobwebs that string the chasm end to end; spun

by Arachnarok spiders, they are thick enough to trap even a gargant. As the grots responsible for his predicament peer over the edge of the chasm, their Spiderfang rivals skitter and crawl from a hundred cracks and fissures. Hekk comes to his senses not a moment too soon – just as the Arachnarok known as Kraka-Bita crawls atop him to deliver a fatal toxin, he tears her fangs clean off and snaps three of her legs before smashing her many-eyed head against the chasm wall. The Spiderfang tribes recede back into the cobwebs, but Hekk's wrath is raised, his state of inebriation making him all but invulnerable to the toxins coursing through his veins. He crawls out of the canyon, his trophy rack boasting Kraka-Bita's tree-trunk legs and a crown made out of bits of giant arachnid perched atop his head. From that day on, both the Brewmasters and the Spiderfang grots of the Crawling Pits call him their leader, and the Spider King is born.

THE LIVING BANQUET
The necroquake screams across the Mortal Realms. It is bad news for every living race, and the gargants are no exception. Taking a sharp blow to the temple from the far-flung projectile of an Ossiarch catapult, the Shyish-born gargant Deaf-ear Darba stumbles into the lands of the Bonereapers' allies in nearby Charnelcourt. He eventually allows himself to collapse, and has a good long lie down amongst the black-barked forests. Weeks later he is awoken by a strange prickling, stabbing sensation across his flanks. Darba opens his eyes to finds himself surrounded by makeshift log-chairs, each of which holds a twisted

hunchback that is literally eating him alive. The delusion-haunted ghouls of the Morgaunt Grand Court had seen his recumbent form as a banqueting table set with a sumptuous feast. Amidst much merriment and ceremony, they had tucked in even as he lay sleeping.

Darba rises to his feet, roaring in pain and fury. He wrenches two trees from the ground and lays about himself with abandon, smashing dozens of ghouls as they gibber and thrash. Yet wounded as he is, bleeding from a hundred minor wounds and missing as many chunks of flesh, he is eventually brought down. The Flesh-eaters of Morgaunt abandon the site, considering the forest to be haunted, and the carrion of the battlefield – including Darba's body – is picked clean. Weeks later a Bonereaper search party finds the site and gathers up the bones, large and small, that lay strewn around the forest. They are put to good use making more crawler-catapults…

OLD ROPEY
On the cursed isle of Decrepita, the wintering tribes speak of Old Ropey in hushed tones. It is rumoured on that benighted isle that a Mega-Gargant of surpassing hideousness roams the night, long ropes of mouldering flesh hanging from his limbs like trail-moss from an elder oak. Those he catches he does not scoop into his cavernous maw, but instead tucks and ties into the loops of rotting muscle and skin that cover his suppurating body, absorbing them as a fungus would absorb the nutrients of a corpse. The legend of Old Ropey reaches the Sylvaneth of Verdia, and at Alarielle's behest, a war party is sent out to slay him. When they reach Decrepita's northern reaches, however, they find not a single living soul – just a trail of rot and curdled, clotted blood leading into the sea.

A NEW ERA
Driven by some unnameable urge to gather together, the Mega-Gargants form tribes and warbands across the Mortal Realms. Bigger than ever before since the death of their father Behemat, their rampage threatens to shatter civilisation entirely.

THE GARGANT TRIBES

Gargants have an innate wanderlust that sees their groupings typically fall apart in disarray, though since the death of Behemat, they have been seen massing in greater numbers. Provided they have enough food, and provided the fiercest of their number keeps the rest in line, they can form rough and ready tribes – for a time.

A gathering of gargants is a spectacular thing, a sight that – once beheld – leaves an indelible mark on the psyche. To one watching from afar, they seem like primordial gods walking out from the mists of time, the true inheritors of the realms. For who could dare to stand against such colossal strength?

The civilised races of the Mortal Realms know of these groupings as 'catastrophes', and with good reason, for the level of devastation these behemoths leave behind them is incredible – they can cause more damage in a single day than an entire army causes over the course of a months-long campaign. The gargants struggle with such complex words as 'cat-as-trophe' and get stuck after the first two syllables. Instead they just call their gathering 'stomps'.

Feet are very important to gargants, for these are the parts of their anatomy with which they interact with the realms most frequently – they love crushing things underfoot and generally revelling in their size and unstoppable brawn. That said, many gargants prefer not to fight against the forces of Chaos, for they tend to wear extremely spiky armour. Trampling a Chaos army can be much like a barefoot human jumping up and down on a bed of nails. Since the feet-maiming devastation of the Sole Wars, some gargants have taken to wearing crude footwear made of the skin of sea serpents or some other extremely tough creature so they can jump up and down on such troublesome foes with impunity.

Gargants save the act of punching things for those times when something tall needs to be knocked down – be it a castle wall or one of the enemy's warbeasts – or when a matter needs to be settled between two of their number. A bare-knuckle brawl or wrestling match is the traditional way to settle a dispute or leadership challenge between gargants, often at the expense of the buildings and landscape features unfortunate enough to be in the vicinity. In times of battle, bending down to smash the enemy with their bare hands is all well and good, but after a while, all that stooping is murder on the back. As a result gargants prefer to just kick things to death, and it is that tendency that informs their view of how a tribe should be organised.

Each stomp is comprised of those gargants that know each other well enough not to fight all the time. Many of them may hail from the same family, bolstered by those gargants that have come to join them over the years. Stomps usually have no more than a couple of dozen members; gargants are a fractious lot, and expecting any more than that to work together is asking for trouble. However, there is a loose hierarchy or 'stomping order' that defines each grouping, and these are based roughly around the shape of a gargant's foot.

The largest or fiercest gargant in the stomp is known as the Big Heel. He is typically a Mega-Gargant, or if not, the largest member of a tribe that has yet to hit the big time. Any other Mega-Gargants in the tribe are said to be 'under the heel' – usually because they lost a fight to their leader – and are expected to go along with the tribe's Big Heel until someone stronger takes his place. It is these massive brutes that form the main bulk of the stomp.

FOLLOWING IN THE FOOTSTEPS OF GIANTS

Mancrusher Gargants that have joined a stomp are known as the Footsloggas. It is they who form the gnarled, leathery toes to the Mega-Gargants' foot. Sometimes these Mancrushers will gather in small groupings of their own, perhaps originating from another group that has been subsumed into the greater stomp. The number of Mancrushers 'toeing the line' under their larger masters varies considerably, just as it is common for gargants to have three toes on each foot, or four, or six, or in the case of Clubfoot Gorg, none at all. This abstraction is not a problem, for gargants can rarely count higher than three.

The reasons that a lesser gargant might hunt out his larger equivalent are many – he could be after better chances of pillage, the chance to sack a large city, or even enlisting aid against an army of comparatively small but dangerous creatures such as Stormcast Eternals or battle-crazed Fyreslayers. Fundamentally, though, all gargants look up to those larger than them. In many ways the tendency to do so is in their bones. When they gather together they adopt something like a familial relationship, even if there is no bloodline linking the gargants in question. The vast ones take the merely huge ones under their wing, albeit grudgingly, and the lesser ones do what they are told to do by the greater ones – most of the time, at least. In this way they form a makeshift alliance; even if the members of the group are not directly related, their proximity (and the looming shadow of the largest and most violent of their number) is enough to force a kind of unity between them that can see a group of gargants fight as a warband for years, or even decades. As such, the ragged tribes of the gargants can have a variety skin tones, trophies and modes of dress amongst them.

RONDHOL STOMP

The gathering of gargants known as the Rondhol Stomp has made its mark on the Ghurish continent of Rondhol. Famously acquisitive, it is led to war by the viciously cunning Kraken-eater known as Bundo Whalebiter.

A stomp that is led by a Kraken-eater is known as a 'taker tribe', where one led by a Gatebreaker is a 'breaker tribe' and one led by a Warstomper is a 'stomper tribe'.

BIG HEEL

The Big Heel is the ultimate authority in the stomp. His raw might and force of personality means that the Mancrusher Gargants under his rule will adopt his favoured culture and tactics (such as they are).

UNDER THE HEEL

The immediate rivals to the Big Heel may be his sons, or be from further afield and simply had it beaten into them that he is the alpha of the stomp. Should the Big Heel show weakness or be badly injured, one of these champions may level a leadership challenge.

FOOTSLOGGAS

Often considered expendable by the Big Heel, the Mancrusher Gargant 'Footsloggas' that go to war in the wake of their leader emulate their alpha in the way they fight.

TOEING THE LINE

Each grouping of Mancrusher Gargants may have its own leader, though he would never dream of challenging the Big Heel to a leadership contest.

MERCENARIES AT LARGE

Gargants of all kinds are given to following their whims; after all, who is going to stop them? Because of this they regularly leave their tribe and fight where and how they please. Of late, Mega-Gargants have been seen fighting alongside the armies of Sigmar, just as they also fight alongside those of Archaon – and even, at times, Nagash.

There are countless gargants across the realms that fight as mercenaries for all manner of paymasters. The more intelligent of their number reason that a constant supply of food and loot is better than the occasional binge, though some will join forces with an army purely for the variety of war it affords them, and others will do it just for the sake of it. But it was not always that way. Once, the gargants of the realms simply gorged themselves whenever they could, and worried about filling their bellies only when their guts were grumbling once more. They had little interest in war, save as a source of good meat. Since the Age of Chaos took its toll upon the landscapes of the Mortal Realms, the gargants have become more cunning in their eating habits, carrying food with them as they travel or ensuring that other people provide it for them. An added perk is the readiness of strong liquor and good ale, something that is never in short supply when paymasters seek the aid of mercenary companies.

It was during a long-standing alliance with the Meatfist Mawtribe that the gargants of Ghur first learned the finer points of the mercenary lifestyle. The Grugg Brothers, a particularly hairy set of triplets from the Ghurish Heartlands, were the first to get the hang of it. They watched the behaviour of their ogor mates whenever they hired out their services in exchange for cartloads of food and drink. In doing so they eventually got their beetle-browed heads around such notions as getting paid, doing what they said they would do the day before, and not attacking the people that had promised to pay them – unless they were really hungry.

Coached over time by the notorious Maneater mercenaries known as the Gutstuffers, the Brothers Grugg learnt notions of strategy and warfare. These included a specific time of attack (usually dawn), the concept of a battle plan (usually writ large in the dirt with a broken stick) and an aftermath in which the spoils of war were shared out (usually, but not always, to the gargants first). Though at first these concepts seemed like a lot of unnecessary bother, their virtues were gradually impressed upon the Grugg Brothers as they walked the Mawpath alongside the ogors.

When they found themselves with more loot than even they could carry after the Meatfists fought a campaign alongside the wealthy Underguts Mawtribe, the Grugg Brothers and their ogor allies went their separate ways. The secrets of the mercenary trade were taken with them to a dozen gargant tribes, and those to a dozen more, passing across shallow seas and through Realmgates until sellsword tactics were integrated across gargant society. It was knowledge passed down through the generations – that sometimes it was better not to eat one of the little squeakers and take his best food, but to fight on his behalf, and be given good meat, ale and treasure over and over again. The notion was so impressive to those gargants that understood the concept it became known as the Great Secret.

Since the Great Secret spread throughout gargant society, the ways in which these behemoths have taken their rewards are many. Those who willingly fight alongside the forces of Order will happily take livestock, not that it stays alive for long. This they will wash down with barrels of mead and firewine. Word has spread amongst gargant society that working for 'the walkin' beards' is always a good idea, for the duardin always pay promptly, and brew exceptional alcohol of all kinds.

The gargants that side with the armies of the undead are reckoned a strange breed even in the devil-may-care society of the gargants. Often pallid and baggy of skin, they subsist mostly on corpses, or perhaps – as in the case of the Lambast Stomp – purely on a diet of bone. These unhallowed terrors are very valuable to Necromancers, vampires, and even the generals of the Nighthaunt processions – for a magic circle of warding that can hold back gheists is no impediment at all to the gargant sent to trample it out of existence.

Those mercenaries that work for the forces of Chaos will likely be fed live meat – disobedient slaves or would-be escapees that are offered to them, or perhaps the warriors that have displeased the warlords of their tribes. Some of the rank and file of the Chaos warband might come to see the gargant in their midst as a demigod of war. There are records of warbands that do not employ the gargant that fights alongside them so much as revere him, making offerings of meat and treasure as a supplicant makes sacrifices to his god. Tying bones and trinkets into his hair and painting his skin with the runes of the god whom they believe has lent them one of his chosen, they chant and scream the brute's name as he smashes their enemies to paste. Though the gargant sees this behaviour as nothing more than an amusing diversion, all too often he finds his body and his mind gradually mutating as the energies of Chaos take hold. The oldest and most experienced of these gargants become truly horrific, walking monstrosities with anatomies that defy all logic and deeds that scar the annals of history.

GARGANT PASTIMES

The rambunctious culture of the gargants often sees younger members of their tribes constantly egging one another on to ever greater feats of stupidity. Being so massive in stature, their youthful sense of invulnerability is challenged only by their tribal elders. When those are absent, they have full rein to cause merry havoc. Contests of climbing, leaping, eating, knocking things down and drinking heavily are perennial favourites. Over the years, more esoteric pastimes have become widespread in gargant society, especially where the ale flows freely. Horse-punting is a simple game to determine who can kick a horse the furthest, with bonus points awarded if the unfortunate beast takes out any unwitting victims upon landing. Boar-scoffing is a similar pursuit, a game where the competitors try to fit as many piglets into their mouths as they can before spitting them all out in a squealing, drool-covered mass. Wakebelching is practised only by gargant mercenaries in civilised lands; they burp as loud as possible into a settlement in the middle of the night and count how many angered sleepers shout in protest in response. The most vociferous objector is usually eaten to teach them a lesson.

Sometimes these dangerous games spread into the field of battle, where the cut and thrust of war adds an extra spice to the drunken antics of these loutish leviathans. Recently, the game of Manskittles has become popular, that activity where a gargant picks up a boulder, dead horse or even a living warrior and hurls it into a pike block or shieldwall to see how many of his enemies he can send sprawling.

Tank-tipping, perhaps the most unusual gargant game of recent years, came to prominence during the Last Charge of Bonn Jensen, when the commodore of Greywater Fastness' famed Iron Squadron drove his prized steam engines straight towards a clan of Mega-Gargants crossing the Verdian Cliffs. Though they took some nasty wounds in the process, the Mega-Gargants rolled each of the Steam Tanks onto their sides, or even upturned them completely. As a result the Mega-Gargants were able to break them apart at their leisure or, in the case of the Warstomper Nagbog and the *Argument of Kings*, lifted above his head and hurled bodily into the sea. Since that day, the rumours that Greywater Fastness has a flying steam tank in its arsenal have proved impossible to dispel.

KRAKEN-EATER MEGA-GARGANTS

Striding from the briny seas come the Kraken-eaters, oldest and gnarliest of all their kind. These lords of destruction feed on sea monsters, and take on the most dangerous foes without hesitation. They prize material possessions above all else, smashing apart entire armies in order to seize new trophies for their lairs.

Amongst the Mega-Gargants of the realms, there are some rare individuals that are long in the tooth, weather-beaten, and even, in the rarest cases, cunning to the point of genuine intelligence. Having seen battles aplenty in their youth, and having eaten their fill of men, duardin, orruks and aelves, they seek the solitude and abundant harvest of the sea. To them, it is enough to sit alone on an outcrop to watch the dawn sun rise or take the weight off their aching joints by submerging themselves in deep water and prowling the coastline. That said, one who impinges on their territory or seeks to plunder their hard-won treasure will be visited with a roaring onslaught that would make a tsunami seem like a splashing puddle by comparison.

Kraken-eaters know their territory like the backs of their grasping hands. Typically, they make their lairs in remote sea caves and abandoned coves known to only the most intrepid sailors. There is a lot to be said for the Kraken-eaters' voluntary isolation; not only does it give them a chance to escape the scourge of Chaos, it also affords them an excellent ambush technique. More than one galleon crew, when sailing into uncharted waters, has mistaken the balding pate of a submerged Kraken-eater for the carapace of a greater shellback or gelatinous tentacloid drifting towards them. Only when the Mega-Gargant rears up, standing to his full height with waterfalls of brine cascading from his torso and his shipwrecka club raised high, does their folly become clear. Moments later their prized vessel is shattered to flinders around them, and they are scooped bodily into the Kraken-eater's yawning maw – for even the strongest swimmer cannot escape when the calloused fingers of these monstrosities are on the grab.

It is not merely the sailors of the Mortal Realms that form the food sources of these ravening titans. Wading or swimming miles from the shore, Kraken-eaters help themselves to the copious sources of sustenance provided by the ocean – from delicious pelagic sealife such as swordfish and sawtooth rays, all the way up to mirror-whales and even the massive sea serpents that slide through the inky depths. Some such prey they seize with their bare hands, snatching bone-armoured blacksharks from underwater currents in much the same manner a trout-fisher might hoist a prize catch from a stream. Even as the beast thrashes they will sink their rotten teeth straight its spine, ensuring it cannot fight back.

The biggest prey of all is that which lends these Mega-Gargants their high status in gargant society; that being the kraken of the black ocean depths. Though few have ever witnessed the sight of a Mega-Gargant wrestling such a beast, it is known for a fact that titanic struggles between gargant and many-tentacled monstrosity take place in the deeps. Many a kraken's bloated and mountainous corpse has been found washed up on a beach with massive gargant bite-marks all over its hide, or with its tentacles literally tied in knots. Some of the grizzled old gargants that prey on these beasts go one step further and flay the leathery hide from these hideous sea creatures, wearing it as a cloak in stormy weather or fashioning protective footwear that allows them to walk across the sharp rocks of the coastline without lacerating the soles of their feet. The latter accoutrements have the added bonus of making it much safer to stomp up and down on a phalanx of aelven spearmen or host of Chaos Warriors, for a gargant hopping around clutching a wounded foot risks toppling over entirely.

BUNDO WHALEBITER

Bundo Whalebiter is a legendary figure across the Coast of Tusks, for he is a Mega-Gargant with a devious intellect. He came into conflict with Idoneth operating out of the Icefang Whirlway when they launched a soul-raid against the same village he was blindly ransacking in search of food. Incensed at the sight of sea monsters 'flying about out of their water', he inflicted so much carnage the Idoneth were forced to flee back into the ocean. Bundo dived into the waves after them, swimming after the glimmer they left in the inky darkness. When he caught up with the light source he found not his quarry, but a hurriedly assembled decoy sent to lead him astray – a lone Fangmora Eel with a glowing jar strapped to its back. Nonplussed, Bundo greedily ate the eel, returning to his lair and wearing the captured artefact as an earring on a whim. Over time, the luminous aetherquartz set into the jar has increased his intelligence to dangerous levels. Since then he has led a series of daring raids ever further inland, and offered his services to a variety of patrons in exchange for ever greater wealth. He has begun a trend that has seen many of his kind adopt similar practices – albeit with wildly differing results, for a jar full of Aqshian etching vitriol or Ghurish eater-wasps hung from the ear can be nothing more than a nasty surprise waiting to happen.

Mega-Gargants of all kinds are territorial. Though the more active ones see those who stray into their domain as a welcome source of food that has saved them the bother of the hunt, Kraken-eaters tend to begrudge the presence of those who might disturb their long, slow thoughts. Some see Chaos invaders much as a hearth-holder might see an infestation of burrowbeasts or iron-eater termites, knowing that if they are left alone to multiply they might one day pose a serious threat. Others are simply highly protective of the trophies they have amassed over the years of carnage, and will attack on sight. The sea caves and pillar-cliffs in which they make their lairs are dotted with treasures taken from shipwrecks and ransacked coastal settlements, amongst them figureheads, crow's nests, the spiralling tusks of sea beasts, chests of jewels, and cannons stacked high. It forms an untidy stash that might look a bit like a mass of broken bric-a-brac to a casual onlooker, but is of great value to the Kraken-eater himself. Those trophies they consider the most precious they will carry with them at all times, lashing them to their backs or even wearing them as ornamentation.

The oldest Kraken-eaters have learned that magic is a powerful thing, for it is a force that cannot necessarily be dealt with using a thirty-foot long warclub. They may even go so far as to hoard magic items and artefacts, tying ensorcelled blades to their waists and wearing arcane objects as ornamentation just as a peasant may wear a silvered crow's foot to ward off evil gheists without quite knowing how or why. In some cases these Kraken-eaters have some manner of magical protection as a result, or even trigger a sorcerous power that enables them to make a passable attempt at magic use. Though the Kraken-eater is almost as likely to harm himself with these magical emanations as his enemies, the novelty of such dabblings in the arcane – and the fact that even a magical detonation is unlikely to fell an elder Mega-Gargant – means that they will keep trying, and perhaps even come to some understanding of how to use the strange weapons they plunder from the treasuries of their victims.

WARSTOMPER MEGA-GARGANTS

Where battle rages fiercest, the Warstompers are drawn to the fray. These monstrosities have become addicted to the din, gore and stink of war, and will cross hundreds of miles in order to 'get stuck in'. So good are they at fighting that flocks of carrion birds follow them wherever they go, eager for the feast of corpses to come.

In battle the Warstompers revel in the sheer power their size affords them. They know full well the fear they can strike into their prey by jumping upon and down on a cohort of elite warriors or smashing a prized warbeast's bones to powder, and they relish the mayhem they cause as the enemy flee in terror.

Warstompers do not take lairs in the manner of Kraken-eaters, nor do they seek specific prey as do the city-crushing Gatebreakers. Instead, they live a nomadic existence, always on the lookout for the telltale smoke and screaming of distant conflict. If they encounter an army before battle is joined, they may well sell their services as a powerful ally. It matters little to the Warstompers who they fight for, so long as they fight either way. They willingly hire themselves out to those who are already on the warpath, and have a healthy respect for the forces of Chaos, whose whole society is based on war. Some amongst them will take payment to fight one foe, only to turn upon their paymasters at battle's end and begin the carnage all over again, laughing with thuggish delight as their former allies flail and scream in denial.

The most cunning Warstompers will actively work towards the continuation of wars that might otherwise come to an end. They will deliberately choose to fight for the side that looks like it might lose in order to prolong the conflict, stamp flat anyone holding the white flag of surrender, or even hunt those honour-guard delegations that cross the wilderness so they never reach their destination and the links of harmony and commerce are never forged. Ultimately, so long as the Warstompers get to enjoy the thrill of battle on a daily basis, they are more or less content.

Warstompers are well versed in the gory craft of war. They know all the best ways to kill their foes, and to defeat the various types of military forces that are likely to be arrayed against them. Should disciplined lines of archers darken the skies with arrows, they will use their clubs to shield their torsos and use a meaty hand to cover their faces, caring not at all if a few shafts pepper their arms and legs. Should an enemy artillery position draw a bead on them, they will pick up a nearby foeman and hurl the screaming unfortunate into the entrenchment in a crude but efficient version of counter-battery fire. Where the enemy forms a shieldwall, they will either jump up and down on it or simply step right over it, kicking out at the back ranks even as the foe tries desperately to redeploy.

Cavalry charges can be lethal to a gargant, for a lance couched at speed with the might of a warhorse behind it can punch through their tough skin – but a Warstomper knows that by stamping down hard and roaring in the faces of such enemies, the steeds may swerve away or even buck their riders. Those who ride mighty drakes or volcanic Magmadroths find the Warstomper's hand around the throat of their warbeast, throttling it and keeping its snapping jaws at arm's length as the Mega-Gargant swings his club hard for the kill. Some Warstompers have even

ONE-EYED GRUNNOCK

One-eyed Grunnock is one of the most famous Warstompers in the realms. Back when he was known as Grunnock Battle-krasha, he attacked the Ossiarch Bonereapers settling Ghurish Necrosia. His assault happened days after the Kharadron Overlords sought to oust the undead from their Ivory Citadel atop its high plateau. At the time of Grunnock's attack, the leaders of the Bonereapers and the Kharadron had reached a stalemate, and begun a treaty. Their pact revolved around the idea that the bones of the land would belong to the Ossiarchs, while the Kharadron would have rights to the aether-gold of the skies. As the two sides were finalising the deal, Grunnock was already climbing the plateau's sheer sides. Atop the cliff he laid about himself with abandon; such was his reach that both sides soon learned to avoid his wrath, but not before he stamped flat the Kharadron Admiral and the Ossiarch Liege even as they were making their final treaty. Grunnock was driven off with an aethershot cannon fusillade that took his eye and split his head open; he fled soon after, but the damage was done. The pact was forgotten, and Ghurish Necrosia is still beset by conflict to this day. As for Grunnock, he has found a dozen new wars since, taking coin from all and sundry and venting the wrath of his skull-splitting headache on any army he can find.

learned to play dead or pretend they are more wounded than they are in truth, feigning a fall or kneeling down to draw the enemy in close before rearing to their full height and unleashing the full measure of their wrath upon the foe.

Warstompers have a tendency to wear trophies as mementos of their most notable victories. Those spears and swords that have plunged deep into their hides they pluck out and keep as talismans so that those weapons cannot hurt them again. Where they can salvage shields or plate metal, perhaps from armoured Chaos beasts or Ironweld war machines, the giants fashion primitive gauntlets of iron and steel that they can use to bat aside the blades and speartips of their prey. Some wear mantles of salvaged wargear, or tusks and horns they have ripped from large and impressive enemies, all the better to increase their intimidating appearance. Though they are ham-fisted craftsmen, they have enough skill and patience to make crude but effective weapons, perhaps lashing a boulder into the end of an ironbark tree or wrenching up a temple pillar with which to crush their prey.

Of late, the Warstompers have found a new and worthy target for their endless aggression – the Stormcast Eternals of Azyr. Wherever columns of dazzling lightning appear on the horizon, the Warstompers break into their signature loping run, heading straight for the area where the gleaming Sigmar-worshippers have come to make their claim of dominance. This will often see them pitching straight into a clash between the Stormhosts and the worshippers of Chaos to fight alongside the warriors of the Dark Gods – not through some predetermined allegiance, but against a mutual foe. Should a Stormcast Eternal be struck with sufficient force it will discorporate, crackling back to the heavens in a blur of energy – though such fireworks are amusing, they leave nothing in the way of a corpse behind on which to snack. At least, reason the Warstompers, the Stormcast Eternals can always be relied upon for a good fight.

GATEBREAKER MEGA-GARGANTS

Gatebreakers have only contempt for the cities and forts of civilised folk. Nothing entertains a Gatebreaker more than shoulder-barging through a castle wall in a tremendous explosion of brick dust, collapsing hundreds of tons of masonry on those sheltering behind and sending those manning the walls tumbling to their deaths.

Most merciless and cruel of all the Mega-Gargants are the Gatebreakers. These are walking siege engines that live to smash their way through the walls of cities, those false havens raised by small fry that think a fancy pile of bricks will keep them safe. Some have even been known to pound the skull-encrusted walls of a Dreadhold to rubble, or to headbutt down the spires and citadels of those architectural marvels raised by aelfkind, proving that, with enough brute force and ignorance, even these mighty edifices can be toppled into the dirt.

The motives that drive Gatebreakers to attack the settlements of the Mortal Realms are threefold. Firstly, being native to areas where Sigmar's new civilisations have begun to take hold, they know there is good eating inside cities – some are even cunning enough to raid, rather than flatten, a new conurbation, leaving enough of it intact that it will recover and gather more defenders to make it a juicier target for the next attack. Secondly, they are driven by the need to show themselves superior to the upstart pipsqueaks that think they can claim the land as their own. Lastly, and perhaps most deeply, they have a grudge against civilised types that can never truly be settled.

On some deep ancestral level these Mega-Gargants know that it was the forces of civilisation that killed their ancestor, Behemat, just as Sigmar the God-King killed Ymnog in his turn. They would gladly kill the God-King if they could, but realise they do not have might enough to take him down – not yet, at any rate. They make do with smashing down the Stormkeeps and ordered districts that human types take such pains to build.

Their claims of ruination are not idle, of course, and are usually backed up by the trappings they take with them on each warpath. Where a rural gargant might wear the pelts and skulls of the great beasts he has slain, the more urban-minded Gatebreakers take their trophies from the cities they take such pleasure in destroying. Temple bells still attached to oaken beams, prized standards that once flew from palace spires, tavern signs from hostelries the ransacker has drunk dry and even gravestones from broken necropolises are lashed to the Mega-Gargant as proof of his prowess. Many wear hoods made of dark leather in imitation of city executioners, those grim figures that dole out the only kind of justice a gargant understands – but where the headsmen take lives, the Gatebreaker ends entire cities. A rune-carved door or enchanted portcullis from a prized gatehouse might be worn as a groin-plate, the reasoning being that where it once protected a city's most valuable area, it now protects that of its conqueror.

In battle, the Gatebreaker tends to wield the masonry and fallen statuary of those civilised areas he has broken apart. He does so not through some sense of pleasing irony in turning the works of men, duardin and aelves against their creators, but simply because they tend to be far heavier and more durable than the tree-clubs favoured by other gargants. When lashed to a heavy chain, a fallen statue can make a devastating flail that can not only batter down walls but also – in those rare circumstances where the gargant's sheer stature is not weapon enough – loop over

BIG DROGG FORT-KICKA

The immensity known as Big Drogg is Shyishan by birth, and has long lumbered across the ravaged lands of Hallost. Where most of that region's gargants have fallen to Chaos invaders, questing Stormcast Eternals or the howling undead released by Nagash's necroquake, not so Big Drogg. The Fort-kicka has a knack for being on the winning side, and has sacked dozens of cities over almost a century of stamping flat anything that irritates him. Of late, Big Drogg has set his sights on truly epic works of wreckage and ruin. He has fought for many a Necromancer and vampire lord; on one memorable occasion, Mannfred von Carstein bribed him to attack an orruk horde from within its ranks in exchange for three barrels of royal blood. Big Drogg was happy to swap sides, for he has a taste for clotted gore. So many corpses has he devoured, in so many stages of decomposition, that he has a severe case of halitosis – his vile, plant-wilting breath is a weapon in itself. Some from the hordes of Destruction call him a turncoat, but they know nothing of Drogg's true agenda. He hopes, by being a regular fixture in the armies of Death, to win the trust of Nagash himself – and clobber him when his back is turned. Only the fates know if he will be resistant enough to the energies of death to make his mark before he meets his long-overdue demise.

the top of the battlements to smash the defenders hiding behind. When wedged between the crenellations, these 'fortcrushas' can then be yanked hard to pull a great section of the curtain wall into rubble, leaving a breach that the giant can quickly exploit.

Gatebreaker Mega-Gargants can often be seen marching alongside the armies of the dead, whether as part of a Necromancer's grave-rabble, a Deathrattle legion or a procession of ghostly Nighthaunts. These opportunist raiders long ago realised that when the undead wish to sack a city, the dead men will kill the inhabitants with cold and tireless determination, but then leave the spoils of war to rot. Not a single terrified oxen or discarded barrel of ale is taken by the revenants; they leave the finest trinkets lying in pools of blood and the larders of kings untouched. Chortling as he picks the remnants of the city's defenders from between his toes, a Gatebreaker will scoop up all of this unwanted bounty and take it back to his lair, returning to the ruined city regularly to harvest as much as possible before carrion strip it bare. He will fill his belly to bursting time and time again, growing strong on the corpses of the slain even as gheists howl through the skies above the broken city.

Though they usually do not realise it until it is too late, these Mega-Gargants can become infected by the energies of death. Their skin becomes paler and saggier, their eyes more hollow, and their need for food and sleep diminishes to almost nothing. Those treasures and trophies they once took such pride in are left scattered across their wake of destruction as they lose their appetite for everything apart from slaughter. To the rest of their kindred, these elder Gatebreakers are unsettling, but never shunned – a gargant is a gargant, and that is all there is to it. If anything, they are welcomed – for though they still seem to take great pleasure in smashing down the walls of cities, these pallid terrors tend leave their share of the food and trophies just lying around in the streets...

MANCRUSHER GARGANTS

It is said that the only thing more terrifying than a wildly raging gargant is a gargant with a sense of purpose. Those gargants that put aside their gluttonous lifestyles to follow their larger Mega-Gargant brethren become far more dangerous, even mastering basic concepts of war as they revel in crushing their foes.

The gargants of the Mortal Realms tend towards indolence and short-sightedness, thinking no further than their next meal unless something angers them enough to embark upon a killing spree. Those that wash their meals of captured livestock and screaming peasants down with a few kegs of stolen ale, or perhaps even a barrel or two of honeymead, get a taste for the sense of giddy invulnerability that floods their system after each feast – not for nothing are they known as Aleguzzlers. The resultant hangover is usually epic in proportion, and though a hungover gargant is amongst the most dangerous and fearsome monsters in the Mortal Realms, he will usually spend the day after in a dank cave, hidden away from the punishing sunlight of Hysh.

However, even the most solitary gargant, upon hearing the rhythmic thunder of a Mega-Gargant on the march, will gather a few dead animals from his cave and follow in his even larger brother's footsteps. He does this quite literally; gargants are very easy creatures to track. Even a badly hungover Aleguzzler can follow the deep impressions left in a Mega-Gargant's wake, knowing that in doing so, he is walking towards the biggest fights of his life.

It may take weeks for a gargant to catch up with one of the largest of his kin, for though Mega-Gargants do nothing hastily, the ten-metre stride of these colossi sees them lumber along at quite a pace. Yet the larger the gargant, the more he needs his sleep. All that pushing over city walls and wrecking galleons can be quite exhausting – and the big ones often sleep for days. A determined gargant can follow the massive dents of each footfall through gale, blizzard and pelting rain, occasionally snacking on those animals and peasants drawn to what they think is an impromptu waterhole, until one day they find their big brothers slumbering away somewhere. At hunt's end it is pretty easy to find a sleeping Mega-Gargant, what with their snore being a ripping, resounding nasal roar that sounds like some manner of stop-start landslide.

Being careful not to disturb their larger cousin's slumber, the gargant supplicant gathers up a clutch of captured food-beasts for breakfast, makes camp, stuffs a wheel of cheese or dead burrowmole in each earhole so he too can get some shut-eye, and readies himself to make common cause in the morning. Despite all this caution he is still likely to make

the same amount of noise as a gore-grunta in heavy armour falling down a cliff. Lucky for them the Mega-Gargants are heavy sleepers, for if a Mega-Gargant is woken prematurely, hungry and enraged, it might kill the lesser gargant just to teach him a lesson.

Should an Aleguzzler succeed in making common cause with a Mega-Gargant after making camp with him, he is given a new sense of purpose. Finally, he has somebody to look up to. He will lope along after the bawling, striding monstrosity he now calls his leader, laughing at the Mega-Gargant's crude jokes and pitching in to attack anything that his master decides is annoying enough to kill. The binges that the gargant once made central to his life are a thing of the past, for the Mega-Gargant takes the lion's share after each battle, and will down a barrel of strong liquor without sharing

KING BRODD

The gargant known as King Brodd hails from the wilderness of the Scabrous Sprawl in Ghyran. He insists that he was never young, and that he is a True Son of Behemat, having crawled full-grown from the chasm known as Titansmawr. There have been those that have challenged that notion in the past, but as they had their brains bashed out in a spectacular display of violence, none have questioned his right to rule the gargants of Verdia. Brodd is exceptionally strong – the skull he wears as a crown came from a mouldragon he killed with his bare hands. Wherever he goes, he carries a huge granite pillar, both his symbol of rulership and his weapon in times of war. The stony artefact was a part of an old Behematian temple, toppled long ago by cyclopean mutants from the crest of Tor Crania – that rounded mountain which in truth was the head of Behemat himself. During the Realmgate Wars, when the Stormcast Eternals sought to free the Scabrous Sprawl from the plague and vermin that assailed it, Sigmar's finest tricked Brodd and his kin into a destructive rampage that did great harm to the schemes of Archaon – though that same campaign later saw Behemat himself slain. Since that day Brodd's gargants have roamed ever further, following their king on the hunt for revenge against those who laid his father low.

anything more than a satisfied belch. This means that even after a battle the former Aleguzzler will stay mostly sober. He gains a new sense of purpose, his mind clearing and his body getting stronger as he fights hard to keep up with his adopted brother. With a new sense of purpose invigorating him, he becomes the kind of gargant known to civilised races as a Mancrusher – a far more dangerous proposition than his inebriated and unruly former self. With his looming patron to drive him on, he is constantly on the warpath.

Where the gargants of the realms gather in tribes, they will hunt out as a group those Mega-Gargants that pass near their territory. The bigger giant is usually happy to have a gathering of such devotees fight alongside him, not least because it fuels his own delusions of godhood and claim to be the next Behemat. Even Kraken-eaters have been known to allow a group of Mancrushers to tag along when they go on the rampage. Becoming nomads, the newly founded Mancrushers are content to exist in the shadow of their larger brethren, and will fight all the harder to impress them.

A tribe of Mancrusher Gargants is able to bring a deadly focus to bear on the battlefield. Rather than their usual habit of stumbling around and tripping over like a bunch of drunken farmhands chasing decapitated chickens, they attack in groups, holding off the counter-assaults of the enemy whilst their leader takes down anything that is even bigger than they are. The presence of a Mega-Gargant – or better yet, several – means that the gargants have finally got a chance to do something really impressive, such as wrecking a city or slaying a truly legendary monster rather than ransacking a tavern or chasing a herd of oxen. More and more are gathered to the living totems that are the Mega-Gargants, until entire tribes of nomadic gargants form, growing ever larger until their footfalls shake the realms and their bellowing charges crush the armies of all those brave enough to face them.

The wrecker gargants of the Harassic Cliffs burst roaring from their galleon-strewn lairs, incensed that such weedy foes as the Idoneth Deepkin dare come after their stuff.

THE VIOLENT COLOSSUS

A tribe of gargants on the rampage inspires true terror. The instinct to flee is all but overwhelming; even the mightiest warlords feel a lump in their throat as the monsters charge in. Here we present a showcase of gargant models expertly painted by Games Workshop's very own 'Eavy Metal Team and Design Studio army painters.

The ruins of Atraxia, once thought defensible against the rampage of the Andtor Stomp, prove little impediment as buildings are smashed down, temples profaned and vital storehouses looted bare.

Kraken-eater Mega-Gargant

Warstomper Mega-Gargant

The Lumberstamps tribe systematically shattered the ancestor-monuments of Krondspine Range, knowing that they would soon draw the vengeful Fyreslayers out of their hold for a proper fight.

The Gatebreaker's contempt for so-called 'strongholds' is not limited to Sigmar's precious civilisations. Even Dreadholds swarming with daemons are smashed to rubble purely to prove the Mega-Gargant mightiest of all living things.

41

Gatebreaker Mega-Gargant

Mancrusher Gargant

Mancrusher Gargant

Addicted to the heart-pounding thrill of battle, a Warstomper willingly seeks out the fiercest prey.
As battle ebbs and flows all around, legends clash amidst the bloodshed, and history is made.

To come to the notice of gargants is a dangerous risk to one and all. Even the fortresses of Nagash's elite, created from iron-hard bone and magic, can be smashed to splinters by a gargant assault.

A TRIBE ON THE RAMPAGE

A gathering of gargants can break an enemy army through sheer muscle, toughness and belligerence. Though the impressive size and power of the models in a Sons of Behemat army means they are more limited in number than a conventional army, there are still several ways you can collect them. We have presented one such way here.

Setting loose a tribe of gargants is an experience like no other. The feeling of indomitability and the temptation to let loose a deep, booming laugh as you crush all before you is great fun. Your opponent will have an excellent time too, with every kill he makes feeling like a deed worthy of legend. Perhaps more than any other army, it is wise to plan out your Sons of Behemat force before you start to build it. How you decide what models to collect will likely be based on the look of the models, as well as how you envision them behaving (well, misbehaving) during a

tabletop battle. Alternatively it might follow a narrative in this battletome or one of your own invention. There is no right way, of course – though you'll need to include at least one Mega-Gargant in your army to lead it (after all, mightier makes rightier!). Depending on which type you use as your general, your tribe will fight in a different way, giving your collection an in-built variety – even when using the exact same collection you can have three distinct gaming experiences. Naturally, we painted up one of each type of Mega-Gargant. We'll be using Bundo

Whalebiter, a Mega-Gargant of the Kraken-eater variety, to act as the leader of our force, thereby bolstering an already formidable line-up with his command trait and artefact of power. Giving him the Glowy Lantern artefact will not only give him a nice shiny trinket to dangle from his earlobe, but also confer a modicum of magical ability (however accidentally he uses it). This will allow us an attempt at unbinding a critical enemy spell if we think it will truly hinder us, and maybe softening up an enemy unit or using Mystic Shield for an extra

measure of protection before the inevitable charge. More importantly, his 'Get Rid of 'Em!' ability will give us a crucial advantage in scenarios that involve claiming objectives. Shifting a trio of Mancrusher Gargants from an objective – with thirty-six wounds between them – can be almost impossible.

Whilst Bundo and his Mancrusher mates concentrate on claiming the objectives to bolster their collection of trophies, his fellow Mega-Gargants will concentrate on smashing the enemy army apart. Big Drogg, our Gatebreaker, will go straight for any enemy units foolish enough to seek protection in cover; because he is so good at destroying such units, his mere presence weakens the foe by forcing them to stay out in the open. The

Warstomper will head straight for the greatest concentration of the enemy infantry, where he can leverage his Titanic Boulderclub to get the maximum number of attacks. The Mancrushers will act as support when needed, tipping the odds in our favour when the Mega-Gargants duel enemy monsters and tying up those units that might outmanoeuvre our force. There is another weapon in our array of tactics that can shift the balance of a game – that of the massive projectiles the gargants can hurl into the enemy. The Hurled Debris, Hurled Boulder and – in the later game – Hurled Body weapons can be devastating, especially when combined to target a single unit. These attacks are a great way to get rid of support characters that use our gargants' large base size against them by skulking between units.

Mega-Gargants
1. Bundo Whalebiter (Kraken-eater)
2. Big Drogg Fort-kicka (Gatebreaker)
3. One-eyed Grunnock (Warstomper)

Mancrusher Gargants
4. Dhobo Skullbreaker
5. Old Greywhiskers
6. Bogda Sharklegs
7. Odo the Strange
8. Unky Hobjaw
9. Mongerbrod the Menace

'We got a job ta do, these days. Wot is it? I dunno. Somefing about stompin' them towns down flat, eatin' up all the pipsqueaks and wotnot. Ask Drogg.'
- Bhodkin Longshanks, Mancrusher Gargant

PAINTING YOUR SONS OF BEHEMAT

Whether you are a veteran brush-wielder with decades of experience or you have never painted a Citadel Miniature in your life, the Sons of Behemat are a real treat to paint. The pages that follow contain some tips and examples to get you started with painting your own tribe of lumbering monstrosities.

A fully painted collection of Citadel Miniatures is a wonderful thing, and a Sons of Behemat army is a force like no other. Essentially it is an army entirely consisting of centrepiece models, each of which is a showcase for your skills. There is real satisfaction to be had in adding colour to your collection, teasing out the finely sculpted details, making your miniatures your own and creating a unified force.

Before painting your models, you'll need to assemble them. To begin with, you should follow the advice in the construction booklet provided with your models, though we have shown some examples of 'kitbashes' in this section for later use.

There's no right or wrong way to go about painting your collection of miniatures. Some people revel in treating each miniature as a work of art, lavishing attention on every millimetre of every model and painstakingly crafting scenic bases. Others prefer a far simpler approach with basic but consistent paint jobs that allow them to quickly get a posse of gargants on the field. There is plenty of middle ground for those that enjoy painting their Mancrusher Gargants but want to devote special attention to their Mega-Gargant leaders. Again, there is no one way to paint, just the way that works best for you. In the end, the goal is to field a fully painted tribe of gargants on the tabletop.

On the following pages, you will find stage-by-stage guides, variant colour schemes and top tips to inspire you as you paint your gargant tribe.

WARHAMMER TV

Warhammer TV's painting tutorials have insights for everyone as they show you how to paint Citadel Miniatures from start to finish. The guides are available for free on games-workshop.com and can also be watched via the Warhammer TV YouTube channel. Why not take a moment to check them out?

DARK FLESH

1. Undercoat the model with Wraithbone Spray. Then basecoat the skin with Catachan Flesh.

2. Apply a heavy drybrush of Bloodreaver Flesh, being careful to avoid the fabric areas.

3. Next, apply a lighter drybrush of Knight-Questor Flesh over the same areas.

4. Apply an even lighter drybrush of Cadian Fleshtone, paying close attention to the face as it will act as the focal point of the miniature.

5. You can give the appearance of dried skin to areas like the face, elbows and knees by adding some fine highlights of Rakarth Flesh.

TOP TIP

You can achieve lighter fleshtones simply by using one of the colours from steps 2-5 as the initial basecoat colour and then going from there. For example, you could start with a basecoat of Bloodreaver Flesh, then drybrush with Knight-Questor Flesh, Cadian Fleshtone and Kislev Flesh. If you want to know what the next lightest paint is for the colour that you are using, you can find out on the *Citadel Colour* app or on games-workshop.com.

DETAILS

Basecoat the eye area with Rhinox Hide and then the eyeball itself with White Scar. Add a dot of Abaddon Black in the centre of the eyeball, leaving some of the white showing at the edges.

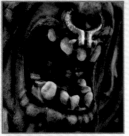

Basecoat the gums with Gal Vorbak Red and the teeth with Wraithbone. Apply a coat of Skeleton Horde to the teeth. Finally, highlight the gums with Tuskgor Fur and the teeth with Screaming Skull.

For grey hair, start with a basecoat of Grey Seer and apply a coat of Basilicanum Grey Contrast paint. Highlight using Grey Seer and then White Scar.

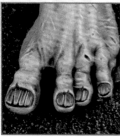

Basecoat with Wraithbone and then apply a coat of Snakebite Leather Contrast paint. Apply some Wyldwood Contrast paint to the bottom of the nail and finish with highlights of Ushabti Bone.

FLESH VARIANTS

Basecoat using Stormvermin Fur, then apply a 1:1 mix of Cygor Brown and Contrast Medium to the recesses. Highlight using Baneblade Brown followed by Karak Stone.

Basecoat with Flayed One Flesh over Corax White Spray. Carefully build up a recess shade using a 1:2 mix of Guilliman Flesh and Contrast Medium. Finish with highlights of Wraithbone and Pallid Wych Flesh.

Basecoat with Kislev Flesh over Corax White Spray. Recess shade using Guilliman Flesh. Finally, highlight with Flayed One Flesh and then Pallid Wych Flesh.

ALGAE-ENCRUSTED TOENAILS

First, basecoat the toenails with Rakarth Flesh.

Apply a coat of Militarum Green.

Apply a shade of Coelia Greenshade.

Highlight with thin lines of Ionrach Skin.

PALE FLESH

1 Undercoat the model with Grey Seer Spray.

2 Apply a coat of Guilliman Flesh and Contrast Medium in a 1:1 mix.

3 Drybrush with Rakarth Flesh using an L Dry brush.

4 Apply a light drybrush of Pallid Wych Flesh, taking care to avoid the recesses.

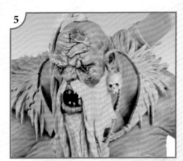
5 Apply a 1:2 mix of Volupus Pink and Contrast Medium into the scars and creases in the brow, and over the nose, lips and bags under the eyes.

TOP TIP

When drybrushing organic surfaces like skin, apply a small amount of paint on the tip of your brush, then take most of the paint off your brush by working the paint off on some kitchen roll. This will help to avoid the paint 'streaking' on the miniature. Remember that 'less is more', and it's easier to add more than take away, so be subtle and delicate for a natural effect.

GINGER HAIR

1 Basecoat the hair with Jokaero Orange.

2 Shade with Reikland Fleshshade.

3 Carefully highlight with Tau Light Ochre.

4 Apply finer highlights of Ungor Flesh.

BONE

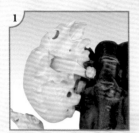

1 Basecoat with Wraithbone.

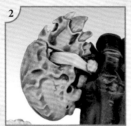

2 Apply a coat of Skeleton Horde.

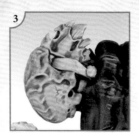

3 Drybrush with Screaming Skull.

TOP TIP
If you need to add more depth and definition, you can apply more Skeleton Horde directly in the recesses of the bone. Because you'll need to be careful not to spill over onto other areas with the colour, using an XS Artificer Layer brush for this would be ideal.

CLOTH

1 Basecoat the fabric patches using Sons of Horus Green, Corax White and Ionrach Skin in any combination you like.

2 Apply a coat of Gryph-charger Grey to the Corax White patches. Apply Coelia Greenshade to the Sons of Horus Green and Ionrach Skin patches.

3 Highlight the Corax White patches with Ulthuan Grey. Highlight the Sons of Horus Green patches with Ionrach Skin. Finally, Highlight the patches of Ionrach Skin with Deepkin Flesh.

4 Pick out the stitches with Wyldwood and highlight them with Karak Stone using an XS Artificer Layer brush.

CLOTH VARIANTS

Basecoat with Steel Legion Drab, shade with Agrax Earthshade, then highlight with Steel Legion Drab and Karak Stone.

Basecoat with Wraithbone, then apply a coat of Fleshtearers Red and highlight with Evil Sunz Scarlet.

Basecoat with Night Lords Blue, shade with Nuln Oil, and highlight with Thunderhawk Blue.

Basecoat with Mechanicus Standard Grey and shade with Nuln Oil. Highlight with Administratum Grey.

MAKESHIFT ARMOUR

Over a Grey Seer undercoat, apply a coat of Akhelian Green to the field of the shield and a coat of Wyldwood to the trim. Then paint the trim with Retributor Armour, leaving the Wyldwood in the recesses, followed by an edge highlight of Stormhost Silver.

Basecoat the shield with Fulgurite Copper. Apply a coat of Gore-grunta Fur all over. Layer the insignia and spikes with Fulgurite Copper followed by an edge highlight of Sycorax Bronze over all the elements of the shield, adding a few thin dashes to look like scratches.

For the red area, apply a basecoat of Khorne Red followed by a recess shade of Black Templar. Edge highlight with Wazdakka Red and then Jokaero Orange. Basecoat the brass area with Fulgurite Copper followed by a coat of Darkoath Flesh. highlighted with Fulgurite Copper and then an edge highlight of Stormhost Silver.

Basecoat Rakarth Flesh, shade Reikland Fleshshade, highlight Rakarth Flesh and Pallid Wych Flesh.

Apply a basecoat of Jokaero Orange followed by a coat of Gryph-hound Orange and Contrast Medium in a 1:1 mix.

With a 2:1 mix of Flesh Tearers Red and Contrast Medium, apply a couple of thin coats towards the bottom of each segment of the shell. Then apply an edge highlight of Jokaero Orange. Paint Wraithbone into the channels between the shell segments, followed by a fine recess shade of Flesh Tearers Red to add definition.

Basecoat with Mephiston Red, shade with Nuln Oil, highlight with Evil Sunz Scarlet and Fire Dragon Bright.

Basecoat with Abaddon Black, edge highlight with Leadbelcher, then add chips with Stormhost Silver.

Basecoat with Stegadon Scale Green, shade with Nuln Oil, then highlight with Russ Grey followed by Fenrisian Grey.

Basecoat with Grey Seer. Apply a coat of Gryph-charger Grey and drybrush with Ulthuan Grey. Use Flesh Tearers Red for the fin.

Wooden Hull: Basecoat with Wraithbone and apply a coat of Wyldwood. Apply some thinned Militarum Green around the broken half and drybrush with Karak Stone.

Horn: Basecoat with Wraithbone, then coat with Skeleton Horde, letting it settle more towards the base of the horn. Highlight with Screaming Skull.

Fur: Basecoat with Grey Seer followed by a couple of coats of Basilicanum Grey. Apply a drybrush of Dawnstone, then Administratum Grey.

DRIFTWOOD

Basecoat using Baneblade Brown.

Shade using Agrax Earthshade.

Highlight with Karak Stone.

Highlight with Screaming Skull.

REPURPOSED CANNONS

Use a combination of Leadbelcher, Iron Warriors and Warplock Bronze to basecoat the cannons.

Apply Agrax Earthshade all over the cannons.

Highlight the silver with Stormhost Silver. Apply a layer of Hashut Copper to the bronze.

Add verdigris to the bronze by using thinned Sotek Green in the recesses. Use thinned Gore-grunta Fur for the rust.

DROWNED BODY

Basecoat with Wraithbone. Then, try to forget you are painting a tiny dead body for recreational purposes.

Apply a thinned-down coat of Gryph-charger Grey (1:2 mix with Contrast Medium).

Paint Druchii Violet into the recesses and in patches to show blood discolouration.

Highlight with Ionrach Skin, paying special attention to the face, hands and feet.

EXTRA DETAILS

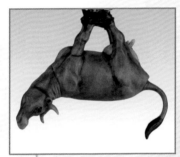

Basecoat with Grey Seer, apply a coat of Apothecary White, then recess shade with Gryph-charger Grey.

Basecoat with Steel Legion Drab, recess shade with thinned Cygor Brown, then highlight with Karak Stone.

Basecoat with Abaddon Black, highlight with Dark Reaper and Russ Grey, then use Stormvermin Fur for the beak.

KITBASHING

The Mancrusher Gargants kit is an extremely versatile kit, but you can personalise it even more with just a few simple cuts. You won't need anything extra for these kitbashes, as they can all be done using only a pair of Citadel Fine Detail Cutters and Citadel Plastic Glue.

COW FLAIL (YES, REALLY)

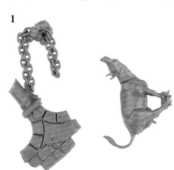

Assemble the archway flail and cow. Using your cutters, carefully clip off the archway where it connects to the chain.

Now, simply glue your cow to the end of the chain and pummel your foes! The leftover archway can be used as a base decoration.

PEG LEG

1

2

Assemble the leg itself and the club with the swords and axes. Cut the club at the hand. Save the hand for a later kitbash (see below).

3

Carefully cut the section with the swords and axes from the club, just before the binding.

4

You'll need to clip the club into a small wedge that will be inserted into the bottom of the trouser leg.

5

Test it after each cut. You should end up with something similar to this that will tuck into the trouser leg.

6

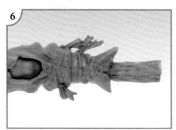

Finally, glue the peg into the trouser leg and tidy up the bottom of the peg if needed.

STATUE CLUB

1

Clip off the gravestone club at the hand (or you could use the hand from the peg leg kitbash, above).

2

Clip off the bottom of the statue club just below the fabric tie.

3

Glue the statue club to the hand, taking care to align it with the club's other side.

PERSONALISED FACES

To make a largely toothless maw, you can easily cut out the teeth of the open-mouthed head variants before gluing the head to the body.

To provide variety amongst your long-bearded menaces, you can cut off the dangling skulls from the bearded gargant.

If you want a really impressive beard, you can trim the centre of the beard and then attach the hair-braid piece to the chin for truly epic facial hair.

THE GARGANT ARMIES

This battletome contains all of the rules you need to field your Sons of Behemat miniatures on the battlefields of the Mortal Realms, including allegiance abilities, a battleplan that lets you stomp all over tiny foes with your gargants, and rules for Mega-Gargant mercenaries. The rules are split into the following sections:

ALLEGIANCE ABILITIES

This section describes the allegiance abilities available to a Sons of Behemat army. The rules for using allegiance abilities can be found in the *Warhammer Age of Sigmar Core Book*.

SONS OF BEHEMAT

Battle traits available to all Sons of Behemat armies (pg 57).

TAKER, STOMPER AND BREAKER TRIBES

Additional battle traits for a Sons of Behemat army depending on the type of Mega-Gargant its general is (see the Lord and Master battle trait, opposite), along with command traits available to the general and artefacts of power available to Heroes in the army (pg 58-63).

BATTLEPLANS

This section includes a new narrative battleplan that pits a Sons of Behemat army consisting entirely of Mega-Gargants against an army of smaller warriors (pg 64-65).

BACKGROUND TABLES

This section contains tables that you can roll on to generate names and quirks for your gargants. You'll find tables for taker, stomper and breaker tribes (pg 66-71).

MEGA-GARGANT MERCENARIES

This section contains rules for including Mega-Gargant mercenaries in armies with different allegiances (pg 72-75).

WARSCROLLS

This section includes the Sons of Behemat warscrolls. These warscrolls take precedence over any warscrolls with no publication date or a publication date earlier than April 2020 (pg 76-79).

PITCHED BATTLE PROFILES

This section contains Pitched Battle profiles for the units in this book (pg 80).

ALLEGIANCE ABILITIES
SONS OF BEHEMAT

BATTLE TRAITS – TITANS OF BATTLE

MIGHTIER MAKES RIGHTIER
Mega-gargants and their followers are so immense that it takes many lesser creatures to drive them from the lands they have claimed.

When determining control of an objective, each friendly **MANCRUSHER GARGANT** model counts as 10 models instead of 1, and each friendly **MEGA-GARGANT** counts as 20 models instead of 1.

Designer's Note: *If the battleplan being played does not follow the normal rules for controlling objectives, you can pick whether to use this battle trait or to follow the rules from the battleplan each time control of the objective is determined.*

CHUCK ROCKS
If a dominant Mega-Gargant spots any Mancrusher Gargants standing around during a battle, he is likely to bellow at them to make themselves useful and start throwing rocks at the enemy!

In your shooting phase, you can pick 1 friendly **MANCRUSHER GARGANT** unit wholly within 18" of your general. Each model in that unit can make a shooting attack with the Chuck Rocks missile weapon below:

Range	Attacks	To Hit	To Wound	Rend	Damage
18"	D3	4+	3+	-1	D3

LORD AND MASTER
Sons of Behemat tribes are always led by a Mega-Gargant, whose traits and foibles will influence the behaviour of their followers.

The general of a Sons of Behemat army must be one of the following types of **MEGA-GARGANT**. Depending on the type of **MEGA-GARGANT** you choose, you can use the extra abilities listed on the pages indicated.

- **KRAKEN-EATER** (pg 58-59). A Sons of Behemat army with this type of general is referred to as a 'Taker Tribe'.

- **WARSTOMPER** (pg 60-61). A Sons of Behemat army with this type of general is referred to as a 'Stomper Tribe'.

- **GATEBREAKER** (pg 62-63). A Sons of Behemat army with this type of general is referred to as a 'Breaker Tribe'.

TAKER TRIBES

BATTLE TRAITS – GREEDY GREAT BRUTES

GET RID OF 'EM!
Kraken-eater Mega-Gargants use their followers in groups to drive off rival claimants to their loot.

When using the Mightier Makes Rightier rule to determining control of an objective (pg 57), each friendly **MANCRUSHER GARGANT** model counts as 15 models instead of 10, and each friendly **MEGA-GARGANT** counts as 30 models instead of 20.

MORE STUFF FOR ME COLLECTION
Kraken-eater Mega-Gargants are avaricious hoarders who love collecting all kinds of baubles and artefacts – even ones that are too small for them to use.

Each time an enemy model with an artefact of power is slain, you can roll for a triumph on the Triumph table. You can use that triumph during the current battle, even if you have already used it. If you do not use it during the current battle, it is lost (you cannot use it in your next battle).

COMMAND TRAITS – IRASCIBLE OLD BULLIES

D6	Command Trait

1 Monstrously Tough: *This Mega-Gargant is incredibly hard to kill.*

This general has a Wounds characteristic of 40 instead of 35.

2 Old and Gnarly: *This Mega-Gargant has so far survived all of the things that the Mortal Realms have thrown at it, and has the scars to prove it.*

You can re-roll save rolls of 1 for attacks that target this general.

3 Louder than Words: *This Mega-Gargant talks rarely, but he carries a very, VERY big stick.*

Add 1 to the Attacks characteristic of this general's Shipwrecka Warclub.

4 Strong Right Foot: *When this Kraken-eater kicks something away, it travels a huge distance.*

When you use this general's Get Orf Me Land! ability to kick an objective marker away, you can roll 3D6 instead of 2D6 to determine how far it is kicked.

5 Very Acquisitive: *This Kraken-eater has collected a vast hoard of magical artefacts.*

You can take 1 extra Trophies Taken By Force artefact of power for this general's army. In addition, this general can have up to 2 artefacts of power instead of 1.

6 Extremely Intimidating: *Nobody wants to get too close to this fearsome Kraken-eater, not even other Kraken-eaters!*

Subtract 1 from hit rolls for enemy models that are within 3" of this general.

ARTEFACTS OF POWER – TROPHIES TAKEN BY FORCE
KRAKEN-EATER MEGA-GARGANT only.

D6   Artefact of Power

1   Jaws of the Mogalodon: *A trophy taken after the slaying of the nine-headed enormity known as the Mogalodon, these give the wearer a bestial, predatory energy that never fades.*

Once per phase, you can re-roll 1 hit roll or 1 wound roll for an attack made by the bearer, or 1 save roll for an attack that targets the bearer. You cannot use this ability to re-roll more than one dice for the bearer in the same phase.

2   Wallopin' Tentacle: *Still writhing long after the original owner's death, the Wallopin' Tentacle can be used as a bludgeon, only to catch up stunned prey in its crushing, rubbery grip.*

At the start of the combat phase, you can pick 1 enemy **HERO** within 3" of the bearer and roll a dice. On a 4+, that **HERO** suffers 1 mortal wound, and you can re-roll hit rolls of 1 for attacks that target that **HERO** until the end of that phase.

3   Jar of Burny Grog: *Though seen as a criminal waste of good liquor, a flask of Aqshian firewater can be smashed over a delicious-looking enemy, instantly setting them ablaze, cooking their flesh and making them even tastier.*

Once per battle, at the start of the combat phase, you can pick 1 enemy unit within 3" of the bearer and roll a dice. On a 2+, that unit suffers D3 mortal wounds and, until the end of that phase, you can re-roll wounds rolls for attacks made by friendly **GARGANTS** that target that unit. On a 1, the bearer suffers D3 mortal wounds.

4   Net of the Beast-reaver: *This enchanted net was stolen from the flagship of a monster-hunting Ulguan Scourgefleet, and has lost none of its potency when it comes to entrapping powerful creatures.*

At the start of the combat phase, you can pick 1 enemy **MONSTER** within 3" of the bearer and roll a dice. On a 4+, until the end of that phase, subtract 1 from hit rolls for attacks made by that **MONSTER**, and you can add 1 to hit rolls for attacks that target that **MONSTER**.

5   Glowy Lantern: *Stolen from the aelves of Hysh after a botched alliance, this aetherquartz jar was at first worn simply because it was shiny – but over time it has increased the intelligence of the wearer.*

The bearer can attempt to cast 1 spell in your hero phase and unbind 1 spell in the enemy hero phase, in the same manner as a **WIZARD**. The bearer knows the Arcane Bolt and Mystic Shield spells.

6   Krakenskin Sandals: *Painstakingly cut from the impervious hide of the legendary sea-behemoth Mejendrokk, these sandals protect the feet of the wearer, allowing him to jump up and down on the enemy without fear of getting spiked.*

The bearer's Almighty Stomp has an Attacks characteristic of 3 instead of 2, a Rend characteristic of -3 instead of -2, and a Damage characteristic of 3 instead of D3.

STOMPER TRIBES

BATTLE TRAITS – BAWLING, BELLOWING LUNKS

GETTING STUCK IN
Warstompers and their followers relish the visceral thrill of battle, and always get stuck in wherever the fighting is most bloody.

Add 1 to the damage inflicted by each successful attack made by a friendly **MANCRUSHER GARGANT** unit that targets a unit with 10 or more models. Add 2 instead of 1 to the damage inflicted by each successful attack made by a friendly **MANCRUSHER GARGANT** unit that targets a unit with 20 or more models.

BIG SHOUTS
Warstompers are constantly bellowing orders to the other gargants under their command.

If your army is a Stomper Tribe, your general must use the following Big Shout command abilities (they cannot use any other command abilities):

Get a Move On, You Slackers!: *The Warstomper yells at his followers to rush the foe.*

You can use this command ability at the start of your movement phase. If you do so, until the end of that phase, if you make a run roll for a friendly **MANCRUSHER GARGANT** unit that is within 18" of your general, that roll is treated as being 6.

Grab Those Rocks and Chuck 'Em at Somethin'!: *Realising that his followers are too far to hit the enemy with their clubs, he shouts at them to hurl some rocks instead.*

You can use this command ability at the start of your shooting phase. If you do so, when you use the Chuck Rocks battle trait (pg 57), you can pick all friendly **MANCRUSHER GARGANT** units within 18" of your general to make Chuck Rocks shooting attacks, instead of only 1 unit.

Oi, You! Yes, You! Charge!: *The Warstomper points a gnarly finger at his lackeys and orders them to attack the enemy.*

You can use this command ability at the start of your charge phase. If you do so, until the end of that phase, you can re-roll charge rolls for friendly **MANCRUSHER GARGANT** units that are within 18" of your general.

Stop Muckin' About and Hit 'Em!: *The Warstomper 'encourages' his followers to focus on bashing at the enemy with every weapon they can muster.*

You can use this command ability at the start of the combat phase. If you do so, until the end of that phase, you can re-roll hit rolls of 1 for attacks made by friendly **MANCRUSHER GARGANT** units that are within 18" of your general.

Watch Yer Backs, You Gormless Lot!: *The Warstomper notices some enemy warriors attempting a sneak attack and bellows a warning.*

You can use this command ability at the start of the combat phase. If you do so, until the end of that phase, you can re-roll save rolls of 1 for attacks that target friendly **MANCRUSHER GARGANT** units that are within 18" of your general.

Where Do You Think You're Going?: *The Warstomper spots some of his minions trying to edge away from a fearsome foe, and gives the shirkers a threatening glare.*

You can use this command ability at the start of your battleshock phase. If you do so, until the end of that phase, do not take battleshock tests for friendly **MANCRUSHER GARGANT** units that are within 18" of your general.

COMMAND TRAITS – VETERANS OF ONE-SIDED BATTLE

D6 Command Trait

1 Monstrously Tough: *This Mega-Gargant is incredibly hard to kill.*

This general has a Wounds characteristic of 40 instead of 35.

2 Old and Gnarly: *This Mega-Gargant has so far survived all of the things that the Mortal Realms have thrown at it, and has the scars to prove it.*

You can re-roll save rolls of 1 for attacks that target this general.

3 Louder than Words: *This Mega-Gargant talks rarely, but he carries a very, VERY big stick.*

Add 1 to the Attacks characteristic of this general's Titanic Boulderclub (to a maximum of 10).

4 Inescapable Grip: *Very few creatures can get away from this Warstomper's grasping fingers.*

When you use this general's Hurled Body ability, you can re-roll the dice that determines if the target is slain and thrown.

5 Very Shouty: *This Warstomper has a voice so deep and loud it can be heard from miles away.*

If this general is on the battlefield at the start of the first battle round, you receive D3 extra command points.

6 Eager for the Fight: *This Warstomper can't wait to get in amongst the foe.*

You can attempt to charge with this general if it is within 18" of the enemy instead of 12". Roll 3D6 instead of 2D6 when making a charge roll for this general.

ARTEFACTS OF POWER – TRAPPINGS OF THE TITAN
WARSTOMPER MEGA-GARGANT only.

D3 Artefact of Power

1 Ironweld Cestus: *This giant gauntlet has been fashioned from the finest metal constructions of the Ironweld Arsenal. The wearer knows well how to use it to block the worst blows of the enemy – and deliver a punishing strike in return.*

You can re-roll save rolls for attacks that target the bearer. In addition, if the re-rolled save roll is an unmodified 6 and the attack was made with a melee weapon, the attacking unit suffers 1 mortal wound after all of its attacks have been resolved.

2 Club of the First Oak: *This immense club heals and invigorates the wearer, even beyond the point of his demise – provided he keeps it in his grip at all times.*

In your hero phase, you can heal 1 wound allocated to the bearer. In addition, if the bearer is slain, roll a dice before the bearer's model is removed from play. On a 4+, the wound or mortal wound is negated and the bearer is not slain, and any wounds that remain to be allocated to the bearer are negated.

3 Mantle of the Destroyer: *This Mega-Gargant's collection of trophies, taken over the course of a years-long rampage, instils him and nearby followers with an unstoppable and monstrous confidence.*

Friendly **GARGANTS** have a Bravery characteristic of 10 while they are within 12" of the bearer. In addition you can re-roll charge rolls for friendly **GARGANTS** that are within 12" of the bearer.

BREAKER TRIBES

BATTLE TRAITS – HATE-FUELLED WRECKERS

BREAKING DOWN THE HOUSES

The followers of Gatebreaker Mega-Gargants adopt the same deep loathing of settlements as is held by their embittered leaders.

Add 1 to the damage inflicted by each successful attack made by a friendly **Mancrusher Gargant** unit that targets a unit that is part of a garrison or is wholly on or within a terrain feature.

In addition, at the end of the combat phase, you can pick 1 terrain feature within 3" of a friendly **Mancrusher Gargant** unit and roll a dice. Add the number of models in that unit to the roll. On a 7+, that terrain feature is reduced to rubble: all of its scenery rules are replaced with the Deadly scenery rule, and its keywords are changed to **Scenery, Rubble**.

FIERCE LOATHINGS

Gatebreakers and their lackeys often have an irrational hatred for certain trappings of civilisation, be it the annoying flag-waving of standard bearers or the irritating pyrotechnics of wizards.

When you pick a Breaker Tribe army, you can choose or roll for 1 ability from the Fierce Loathings table. The ability applies to friendly **Gatebreaker Mega-Gargants** and friendly **Mancrusher Gargant** units.

D6	Fierce Loathing
1	**Bossy Pants and Clever Clogs:** *What is it with pipsqueaks bossing others about, and pointing at stuff and making it blow up? It ain't clever, it's stoopid!* Add 1 to hit rolls for attacks made by units with this ability that target a **Hero** or **Wizard**.
2	**Idiots with Flags:** *How come these runts think you can stake a claim with a posh flag? It don't mean nuffin!* Add 1 to hit rolls for attacks made by units with this ability that target a **Totem** or a unit with any command models.
3	**Shiny 'Uns:** *Why do these tinies think dressing up in shiny metul and strappin' on shields means they can't be hurt? Teach 'em a lessun!* Add 1 to hit rolls for attacks made by units with this ability that target a unit with a Save characteristic of 1+, 2+, 3+ or 4+ and that is not a **Hero** or **Monster**.
4	**Crowds:** *What is it with these little gits getting together in big crowds, yellin' and shoutin' and acting all tough? They ain't tough, they're dumb. Easier to kill 'em all at once!* Add 1 to hit rolls for attacks made by units with this ability that target a unit with 20 or more models.
5	**Wannabes:** *So they think that being as big as us makes 'em just as fighty? Time to cut 'em down ta size.* Add 1 to hit rolls for attacks made by units with this ability that target a **War Machine** or **Monster**.
6	**Piggybackers:** *What is it with these squeakers that think riding around on a good meal makes 'em 'arder?* Add 1 to hit rolls for attacks made by units with this ability that target a unit with a mount and that is not a **Monster**.

COMMAND TRAITS - UNSTOPPABLE BESIEGERS

D6	Command Trait

1 Monstrously Tough: *This Mega-Gargant is incredibly hard to kill.*

This general has a Wounds characteristic of 40 instead of 35.

2 Old and Gnarly: *This Mega-Gargant has so far survived all of the things that the Mortal Realms have thrown at it, and has the scars to prove it.*

You can re-roll save rolls of 1 for attacks that target this general.

3 Louder than Words: *This Mega-Gargant talks rarely, but he carries a very, VERY big stick.*

Add 2 to the Attacks characteristic of this general's Fortcrusha Flail.

4 Extremely Bitter: *This Gatebreaker has a particularly deep and abiding hatred of the trappings of civilisation.*

You can choose or roll for 2 abilities from the Fierce Loathings table (pg 62) for your army instead of 1. If you randomly generate the second, roll again if it is the same as the first. The second ability only applies to the general.

5 Smasher: *There is nothing this general likes more than reducing buildings to rubble.*

When you use this general's Smash Down ability, you can re-roll the dice roll that determines if the terrain feature is turned into rubble.

6 Sees Red: *The mere presence of a settlement infuriates this Mega-Gargant so much that they simply ignore any wounds they have suffered.*

While this general is within 9" of a terrain feature that can have a garrison, when you look up a value on this general's damage table, they are treated as if they have suffered 0 wounds.

ARTEFACTS OF POWER - LEGACY OF DEMOLITION
Gatebreaker Mega-Gargant only.

D3	Artefact of Power

1 Enchanted Portcullis: *The metal gate that once barred entry to the South Tower of Excelsis bears a potent spell of repulsion. Repurposed as armour, it now serves to protect the wearer's 'vulnerables' from harm.*

Roll a dice each time you allocate a wound or mortal wound to the bearer. On a 6, that wound or mortal wound is negated.

2 The Great Wrecka: *This gigantic masonry-and-chain combination has had potent curses of death and destruction laid upon it by malignant shamans. All things bludgeoned by its weight will crumble to dust – be they fortress, or be they living creature.*

If the unmodified hit roll for an attack made with the bearer's Fortcrusha Flail is 6, that attack inflicts 1 mortal wound on the target in addition to any normal damage. In addition, when you use the bearer's Smash Down ability, you can add 1 to the dice roll that determines if the terrain feature is reduced to rubble.

3 Kingslaughter Cowl: *This dark leather hood has been handed down through generations of city-wrecking Mega-Gargants who have made it their business to hunt down and crush upstart kings, queens and warlords across the realms.*

You can re-roll wound rolls of 1 for attacks made by the bearer that target a **Hero**. In addition, you can re-roll wound rolls for attacks made by the bearer that target a general.

BATTLEPLAN
A FORLORN HOPE

The immense gargants had loomed into sight hours before, their silhouettes stark against the horizon. They had been the bane of the region for months. Now, on this sacred ground, a last stand would be taken. No more would the people huddle in their fortress, waiting for the walls to be cast down upon them. Here they would take the fight to the giant brutes that had bled the lands white. Here they would stand, and in all likelihood, here they would die.

In their simple-minded arrogance, the gargants cared not for traps, nor preparedness. The best of the best had been massed to take them on; though few in number compared to the legions that once marched from this proud province, they were rugged survivors one and all. As the gargants roared their challenges, storming forward to begin the slaughter, not a single soul took a backward step.

THE ARMIES

One player is the Sons of Behemat player, and their opponent is the Forlorn Defender. The Sons of Behemat player must use a Sons of Behemat army that consists of either 1, 2 or 3 MEGA-GARGANTS. The Forlorn Defender's army can be from any Grand Alliance or faction. The army must have five units for each MEGA-GARGANT in the Sons of Behemat army. Each unit in the army must conform to one of the unit types from the following list:

Horde Unit: A unit of up to 20 models, each with a Wounds characteristic of 1 and a Save characteristic of 6+ or '-'.

Regular Unit: A unit of up to 10 models, each with a Wounds characteristic of 1 and a Save characteristic of 3+, 4+ or 5+.

Elite Unit: A unit of up to 5 models, each with a Wounds characteristic of 2 or 3.

Guard Unit: A unit of up to 3 models, each with a Wounds characteristic of 4 or 5.

Champion: A HERO that is not a MONSTER.

OBJECTIVES

The players roll off, and the winner decides which territory each player will use. The territories are shown on the map.

The Forlorn Defender must then set up 3 objectives. In this battle, each objective is of a different type. The Forlorn Defender must say which type of objective each one is as they are set up. Each objective must be set up more than 12" from the edge of the battlefield and more than 18" from any other objectives.

Treasure Trove: This collection of artefacts is treasured by the Forlorn Defenders and greatly desired by Kraken-eater Mega-Gargants.

Fighting Ring: This circle of bloodied ground is used by the Forlorn Defenders as an arena, making it an irresistible lure to any Warstomper Mega-Gargant.

Monument: This statue of a heroic champion is revered by the Forlorn Defenders and loathed by Gatebreaker Mega-Gargants.

SONS OF BEHEMAT TERRITORY

FORLORN DEFENDER'S TERRITORY

SET-UP

The players then alternate setting up units one at a time, starting with the player that won the roll-off to determine territories. Units must be set up wholly within their territory, more than 12" from enemy territory. Continue to set up units until both players have set up their armies. When the Sons of Behemat player has finished setting up their army, the Forlorn Defender must set up the rest of the units in their army, one after another.

FORLORN BUT UNYIELDING

The defenders know that they will have little chance to survive the coming battle, but they are determined to sacrifice themselves if it means that their kingdom can be protected from the depredations of the rampaging Mega-Gargants.

Do not take battleshock tests for Forlorn Defender units while they are wholly within 12" of an objective.

BATTLE LENGTH

The battle lasts for 5 battle rounds.

GLORIOUS VICTORY

The player with the most victory points at the end of the battle wins a **major victory**. If both players have the same number of victory points, use the tiebreaker to determine which player wins a **minor victory** or if the battle is a **draw**.

VICTORY POINTS

Each player scores 1 victory point at the end of each of their turns for each objective they control.

The Sons of Behemat player scores 2 victory points instead of 1 for an objective they control if there is a MEGA-GARGANT of the appropriate type within 3" of it, as follows:

Treasure Trove: KRAKEN-EATER

Fighting Ring: WARSTOMPER

Monument: GATEBREAKER

TIEBREAKER

If the players are tied on victory points at the end of the battle, then the Sons of Behemat player scores 1 kill point for each Forlorn Defender unit that has been destroyed, and the Forlorn Defender scores 5 kill points for each MEGA-GARGANT that has been slain.

If one player has a higher kill point total, they win a **minor victory**. If neither player has a higher kill point total, the battle is a **draw**.

TAKER TRIBE BACKGROUND TABLES

Kraken-eaters and their ilk are not too bothered what people call them, so long as they are left alone. Still, they typically earn impressive names earlier in their lives, and regardless of their motivations for going to war, their combination of strength and cunning makes them inspirational leaders to the taker tribes in their wake.

Alroy Leihan, bosun of the White Courser, felt his ravaged back scrape against barnacle-encrusted iron. At high tide, he would be buoyed up to the top of the cage, and the cage to the top of its cave-hollow. He was submerged anew by each wave; around him bobbed the rotting, swollen corpses of those of his crewmates who had failed their trial by water, drowned by the battering, suffocating tide. Some of them he had killed himself, effectively, elbowing them aside or climbing atop them in his desperation to get a lungful of sweet air instead of choking brine. Ironic, then, that he should seek to dive so deep when the brute returned.

'It's here,' said Jedro, the second cannoneer. The young man's voice was filled with terror, his eyes wide as the sunlight was blotted out by an immense silhouette. The monster stooped low and came into its lair. Alroy saw its midriff, girded with wreckage, the blindfolded figurehead of the Courser strapped to its hip. He took a deep breath and dived down, trying desperately to evade the creature's notice as its vast, grasping hand opened the heavy cage. Jedro dived too, hiding under the swollen corpses. He was a moment too slow. Giant fingers burst through the water in serpentine trails of bubbles, closed around the cannoneer, and squeezed.

Jedro burst. A blackish-green cloud filled the water, red where the sun's last rays shot through.

Alroy screamed, and felt his lungs burn as some primal instinct forced him to surface. The bloody, gaping maw of Fimnog Sea-crawler was the last thing he ever saw.

You can use the tables on these pages to generate first names, last names and quirks for your gargants. There are three tables for each category. When rolling for a category, first roll a D3 to determine the table you will use, then roll a D6 to generate the result. Alternatively, you can simply pick the result you like the best.

D6	FIRST NAME
1	Old Moggor
2	Berdo
3	Drabb
4	Soggdur
5	Gurge
6	Fergun

D6	LAST NAME
1	Sea-drinker
2	the Briny
3	Puke-breath
4	Salt-hand
5	Cannon-chucker
6	the Elder

D6	FIRST NAME
1	Fimnog
2	Kraggi
3	Gargolo
4	Long Dorg
5	Krong
6	Slimy Sollo

D6	LAST NAME
1	Gulleygash
2	the Hoon
3	Sea-crawler
4	Creekprowl
5	the Krokodon
6	Whale-gobbler

D6	FIRST NAME
1	Zongro
2	Nodge
3	Boghade
4	Modo
5	Odd Viggo
6	Glardy

D6	LAST NAME
1	Tide-shouter
2	the Wrinkled
3	Sea-swill
4	the Thinker
5	Marlinspike
6	Net-hurler

D6	QUIRK
1	**Filthy:** Swilling around in the tidal muck has made this gargant's stench particularly odious. His legs are thoroughly encrusted with the black, stinking slop of his native mud flats.
2	**Exceptionally Surly:** This gargant's temper would sour milk. Negotiating with him triggers a volley of bellowed and highly offensive insults, levelled at deafening volume.
3	**Thunderstruck:** This gargant has been literally struck by lightning, yet lived to tell the tale. Other than his scorch marks and a profound lack of hearing, the heavenly bolt has slowed him not at all.
4	**Whale-slayer:** This mighty warrior busies himself only with large, impressive kills. He makes a beeline for the war beasts and bound monsters of the enemy, hoping to add another notable death to his tally.
5	**Impervious to the Elements:** Weather-beaten, storm-tossed and with a nasty case of frostbite, this gargant pays no mind to the lashing of rain and sleet. Worse things happen at sea, after all.
6	**Greedy:** There is no end to the grasping, grabbing avarice of this gargant. On the field of battle, he will usually go after the enemies with the most shiny and impressive loot.

D6	QUIRK
1	**Miserly:** Even amongst the Kraken-eaters of the coast this gargant is considered stingy; though he wears bags of gold and carries treasure to war, he would never consider actually spending it.
2	**Fishy Stench:** This gargant feeds almost exclusively on the bounty of the sea, and is a very messy eater. His skin is covered in a disgustingly pungent sheen of sweat and fish oil.
3	**Boggle-eyed:** Some facet of coastal life – and generations of inbreeding – has given this gargant bulbous and protuberant eyes as well as a pallid, cold cast to his skin.
4	**Strangler:** This gargant prefers to throttle larger prey to death, and is not above using a disembodied tentacle as a garrotte, or wrapping his net around his enemy's throat to better cut off their air supply.
5	**Gimped:** This gargant has a dodgy leg, whether through old age, or maybe through having his thigh all but bitten through by a Mogalodon or some other nautical terror. He still gets about at quite a rate.
6	**Coastal Guardian:** This gargant has a long-standing alliance with a powerful port-city or equivalent, and is even considered relatively civilised by his fellows, though none would say that to his face.

D6	QUIRK
1	**Boat-biter:** This gargant has acquired a taste for driftwood, and will happily eat his way through an entire shipwreck if he gets the chance. There is little he cannot chomp his way through as a result.
2	**Corpse-dangler:** The gargant has a fondness for dangling the rotting corpses of slain enemy generals and people of importance from his person, just to see the looks on his appalled victims' faces.
3	**Shanty-singer:** The gargant sings bawdy sea shanties he learned from captured sailors, off-key and at ear-splitting volume. Sometimes he even does the actions. It is not a pleasant sight.
4	**Sharkskin-clad:** The gargant wears the skin of some colossal shark as a cloak or mantle, its jaws around his shoulders to give him an even more fearsome appearance.
5	**Headtaker:** The gargant prefers to grab people up in his meaty fist, then bite their heads clean from their necks in a spray of gore. Sometimes he then spits the disembodied head at his enemies.
6	**Terrifying Reputation:** Stories are told far and wide of this gargant ripping the limbs from his victims, dragging them across sharp coastal rocks and committing all manner of barbarities before his meal.

STOMPER TRIBE BACKGROUND TABLES

The Warstomper Mega-Gargants that hunt and destroy the armies of the Mortal Realms are often driven by a cruel sense of superiority. They and their kin take boastful names that speak of those great deeds they have accomplished, much as Behemat did before them – the exact meaning is not important, as long as it sounds good.

Tharnwaen rode his dark-skinned steed hard out of the canyon. The stink of the war beyond was thick, the sounds of battle close. He would be first into the fray. He would be first to loose the killing fire; first to bring down the sweaty barbarians they had trapped.

No escape. No mercy.

The aelven warlocks emerged from the chasm to see the horn-helmed humans fighting the slaughter-cults up ahead. Suddenly Tharnwaen's steed reared, whinnying in terror, those of his fellows bolting around him. A colossal giant barrelled towards them from the left, lank hair flapping as its feet slammed into the dirt. 'Meat!' it shouted, its voice a gravelly rumble. 'Meat for Gongar the Red!'

Leaping forward in his saddle, Tharnwaen kneed his steed hard, forcing it to stumble under the monstrosity's club as the tree-trunk sized weapon swung around. It caught three of the warlocks behind him as they fled, sending the horses tumbling away. Two of the aelf riders leapt free, but the third was crushed under his steed's corpse. The survivors let fly a volley from their hand crossbows, peppering the gargant's forearm. The club swung in low regardless. This time Tharnwaen spurred his steed to leap clear over it and bolted for safety. He glanced back to see the giant jumping high, its colossal bulk eclipsing the sun for a moment. Then it stamped back down with meteoric force. Tharnwaen was thrown from his steed, breaking his leg on a sharp rock. The beast leered down, its grasping hand reaching. No escape, thought Tharnwaen. No mercy.

You can use the tables on these pages to generate first names, last names and quirks for your gargants. There are three tables for each category. When rolling for a category, first roll a D3 to determine the table you will use, then roll a D6 to generate the result. Alternatively, you can simply pick the result you like the best.

D6	FIRST NAME
1	Nonko
2	Lunk
3	Norgon
4	Belko
5	Lobdor
6	Orr-drog

D6	LAST NAME
1	Drakebreaker
2	Lumberfist
3	Warcrusher
4	Godthump
5	Kingstomper
6	the Red

D6	FIRST NAME
1	Daggran
2	Adog
3	Nogar
4	Hroff
5	Stampr
6	Drungo

D6	LAST NAME
1	Bouldercatch
2	Gravenbelly
3	King of Goliaths
4	Stalebreath
5	Hornmantle
6	Cloudsniffer

D6	FIRST NAME
1	Gongar
2	Varbo
3	Angrudd
4	Dolgolp
5	Wohrag
6	Bulg

D6	LAST NAME
1	Linebreaker
2	Redreaver
3	Iron-shins
4	Horse-hurler
5	Flag-stealer
6	the Bellower

D6	QUIRK
1	**Big Game Hunter:** The gargant has a fixation with taking down the widest variety of beasts he can manage before he dies. This has earned him a lot of claw-mark scars and a mad glint in the eye.
2	**Snowbeard:** This gargant has been smashing, marauding and killing for centuries, and his beard is white as the mountain snow – except for those times when it is matted with clotted blood, of course.
3	**Carrion Wake:** The many corpses this monstrosity leaves behind as he slaughters his way across the realms mean that he is perpetually followed by carrion birds and opportunistic scavengers.
4	**Totem of the Greenskins:** Whether he likes it or not, this gargant is a totem of strength and ferocity to the local greenskin tribes, and they chant and holler in thuggish glee whenever his club starts swinging.
5	**Shatterer of Shieldwalls:** To this gargant, a tightly formed shieldwall is a challenge. He takes great pleasure in kicking orderly formations into sprawling, panicking anarchy.
6	**Counter of the Dead:** Unusually for one of his kind, this gargant has learned to count without using his fingers. As he kills, he counts – and when he reaches ten, he starts all over again, but a little bit louder.

D6	QUIRK
1	**Clubsmith:** The gargant takes great care in the construction of his weapons. His club's current incarnation is solid and heavy enough to break a cavalry formation without a single loose binding.
2	**Blessed by the Bad Moon:** Having fought alongside many Moonclan grots, and perhaps even Skragrott himself, the gargant is covered in many a fungal growth. Their spores inure him to pain.
3	**Ravenous Appetite:** Since he triumphed in an eating competition against a local mawtribe's tyrant, the gargant has an entourage of Ghurish ogors who believe him to be a prophet of the Gulping God.
4	**Carnage Personified:** So long as there are living things within hitting distance, this gargant never stops killing. Even those who worship him from afar know to keep their distance.
5	**Tough as Old Boots:** The gargant has leathery, weather-beaten skin so tough that only the sharpest blades can hope to slash through it.
6	**Maneater Eater:** After a deal involving a group of ogor mercenaries went badly wrong, the gargant has developed a taste for ogor flesh. He'll still fight alongside them, but only so he can get close…

D6	QUIRK
1	**Bestial Curse:** This gargant has been cursed by a Darkoath enchantress to speak only in the guttural growls and yipping howls of rabid wolves. He ensures that his actions speak louder than words.
2	**War-shouter:** To say this behemoth is loud is an understatement. He uses his voice as a weapon, and he constantly roars oaths and insults at the runtish races that scurry around his ankles.
3	**Vindictive:** One who makes this gargant bleed is fixed with a steely gaze, even if it is from a hundred metres away – he will prioritise that individual's destruction over all else until the insult is avenged.
4	**Arrow Magnet:** The gargant has been pin-cushioned by so many arrows in so many battles that he barely registers their impacts any more. He has an especial hatred for archers nonetheless.
5	**Totem of the Chaos Tribes:** The worshippers of the Dark Gods see this gargant as a savage incarnation of the Ruinous Powers. He even allows them to paint their runes of power on his skin before battle.
6	**Besotted by War:** The thrill of battle has addled this gargant's mind, whether through the intoxicating effects of a nearby Waaagh! or the sheer adrenaline of life-or-death struggle. Best not to get close.

BREAKER TRIBE BACKGROUND TABLES

Gatebreakers are often concerned with their reputation, and will often cultivate impressive names or epithets that speak of their notable victories. For the Gatebreakers, actually remembering these names is the difficult part. They may allow a grot or two to act as their herald, ensuring all those good victories do not go to waste.

'*Reload and fire again, idiots!*' Herbot Grondervale swore into his beard, his frustration and despair rising. The monstrosity was bleeding from a dozen nasty wounds; so far the Greywater-trained garrison had hit it with two Helblaster volleys, and after a direct hit from a rocket battery, fire trailed like a mantle from its burning cowl. Yet it was still splashing through the swamp so fast it would reach the walls before they could fire again.

The gunner sergeant told himself to have faith. They had dug a stake-studded pit behind the fort's gate for good reason, working ceaselessly overnight after the patrols got word from captured grots that Vongo the Besieger was going to pay them a visit. And then there was von Marlke. Surely there was no way the sniper could miss.

Sure enough, as the brute's loping run broke into a charge, one of its eyes disappeared in a spray of crimson. It stumbled, no doubt hoping to smash the gate in its death throes.

Grondervale's triumphant grin disappeared as the gargant shouldered right through the wall to the right of the tower gate in an explosion of rubble. Roaring, it brought its flail down on a knot of guardsmen. An explosion of gore, and all that was left was scattered limbs and strewn intestines. '*Pivot and shoot! Kill it!*'

As he hauled at the closest Helblaster, the monster's single eye glared balefully right at him. It picked up a chunk of masonry the size of an ox-cart and threw it hard. On instinct, Grondervale ducked behind the volley gun. The boulder crashed in, and he died anyway.

You can use the tables on these pages to generate first names, last names and quirks for your gargants. There are three tables for each category. When rolling for a category, first roll a D3 to determine the table you will use, then roll a D6 to generate the result. Alternatively, you can simply pick the result you like the best.

D6	FIRST NAME
1	Boggro
2	Zung
3	Big Gorg
4	Luggor
5	Nogar
6	Vongo

D6	LAST NAME
1	Shatterer of Axton
2	Breaker of Targuard
3	Eater of Dunnstag
4	the Boulder-breaker
5	the Besieger
6	the Moat-drinker

D6	FIRST NAME
1	Nong
2	Bode
3	Donad
4	Odo Garg
5	Fodrog
6	Borro

D6	LAST NAME
1	the Thug of Redkeep
2	the Rubble-maker
3	Batterer of Dinstown
4	the Cowled Destructor
5	the Death of Urn City
6	Smasher of Galeston

D6	FIRST NAME
1	Jurt
2	Oidor
3	Guddro
4	Derrock
5	Porrod
6	Uggar

D6	LAST NAME
1	the Eater of Fortresses
2	the Bell-cracker
3	the Bane of Empires
4	Flattener of Urdenstag
5	Killer of Neuhaim
6	Demolisher of Norde

D6	QUIRK
1	**Hatred of Temples:** The idea of runty little idiots worshipping some runty little god offends the gargant to the point he seeks out and destroys places of worship whenever he can.
2	**Punch Drunk:** This gargant has taken a battering from enemy artillery as he single-handedly stormed the walls, and it's left him dazed, confused, and fatally unpredictable.
3	**Seething:** Whilst kicking over a city wall this gargant broke one or several of his toes, and he's not happy about it. Naturally it is the fault of the citizens for building such a stupid wall in the first place.
4	**Spire-toppler:** The gargant thinks that tall, thin buildings are particularly offensive, and must be cast down – if not by a well-hurled chunk of rubble, then hacked down much as a lumberjack fells a tree.
5	**Fiendish Hunger:** The gargant will prioritise feeding even over smashing things to a pulp. Those citizens he grabs up from the streets are usually thrust straight into his maw then and there.
6	**Deathly Pallor:** This gargant is pale to the point of albinism, more because of his habit of avoiding the sun's rays and hanging around with the armies of undeath than any particular accident of birth.

D6	QUIRK
1	**Not Quite Alive:** This gargant died in battle some time ago, which accounts for the dire smell and the organs spilling out of his guts. Luckily, his necromantic allies were close by to get him back on his feet.
2	**Hunter's Eye:** Running and hiding is no defence against this brute. He has a knack for ferreting out his prey – any who seek shelter quickly find it brought down around their ears before he snatches them.
3	**Killer Instinct:** With a knack for knowing when to strike, this gargant is a true killer; none can hope to get past him without being crushed or receiving a fatal wound.
4	**Wrecking Ball:** Like some titanic Moonclan Fanatic, this gargant swings his fortcrusha flail around him in sweeping two-handed motions that can smash a fortified keep to scattered rubble in minutes.
5	**Living Siege Engine:** The gargant deigns to let his allies climb atop his shoulders, whether clinging to his cowl or upon a ramshackle structure, so they can gain the walls swiftly as he goes to siege.
6	**Storm-hater:** The only creatures to ever best this gargant were Sigmar's shiny gold warriors. Ever since, he has had a powerful loathing for the Stormhosts – and even the thunderheads that carry them.

D6	QUIRK
1	**Very, Very Drunk:** Raiding sixteen taverns in a row and guzzling the barrels within has proven too much even for this behemoth's constitution. A drunken gargant can be even deadlier than a sober one.
2	**Graverobber:** The gargant has a fondness for eating corpses, and will seek out graveyards wherever he raids, delving meaty hands into the earth to yank up tasty cadavers as a Ghyranite farmer does potatoes.
3	**Portcullis Collector:** Something about portcullises entertains this gargant – perhaps it's the fact that when used as an improvised weapon, they can impale half a dozen pipsqueaks at the same time.
4	**Superstitious:** Unlike the vast majority of his kind, this gargant took the omens of the Time of Tribulations seriously. He wears many lucky charms and fetishes to ward off the attentions of Nagash.
5	**Doom Crier:** The gargant once saw a town crier at his task of professional shouting. Now the big lunk does much the same, ringing a temple bell and proclaiming the doom he brings to those around him.
6	**Realmgate Smasher:** The civilised races consider it incredibly dangerous and foolhardy to attack a Realmgate, for the magical backlash is incendiary. This gargant cares not at all, and does it anyway.

MEGA-GARGANT MERCENARIES

This section contains rules that allow any army to include a Mega-Gargant mercenary, as well as additional rules for Kraken-eater, Warstomper and Gatebreaker Mega-Gargants that are used when they are taken as mercenaries.

To include a Mega-Gargant mercenary in your army, you must first pick which Mega-Gargant mercenary your army will hire from pages 73-75. Any army can include a Mega-Gargant mercenary, not just Sons of Behemat armies.

You can hire 1 Mega-Gargant mercenary for your army. If you do so, your army cannot include any other mercenary units or any allied units. The players can agree to ignore these restriction in open and narrative battles.

Mega-Gargant mercenaries gain the **Mercenary** keyword. **Mega-Gargant Mercenary** units are treated as part of your army, except that they are not included when working out your army's allegiance, and can therefore be part of a different Grand Alliance or faction from the rest of your army. In addition, a **Mega-Gargant Mercenary** unit cannot be the army's general, and cannot use or benefit from your army's allegiance abilities.

PITCHED BATTLES

You can include 1 **Mega-Gargant Mercenary** unit in a Pitched Battle army, even if it costs more points than you have available to spend on allied and mercenary units. A pitched battle army can never include more than 1 **Mega-Gargant Mercenary** unit.

Mega-Gargant Mercenary units are not included when working out the number of Battleline units in your army, but they do count towards the maximum number of Leader and Behemoth units that can be included in your army.

MERCENARY SPECIAL RULES

If you include any **Mercenary** units in your army, the following rule applies during the battle:

Disruptive Presence: *Even the most well-ordered fighting force will be disrupted by the arrival of mercenaries, presenting a unique challenge to the army's general.*

If your army includes any **Mercenary** units, at the start of your hero phase in the first battle round, you do not receive 1 command point.

Designer's Note: *If you want to use a mercenary Mega-Gargant in your army but want it to be one of your own invention with a different name, feel free to use the rules on one of the following pages to represent them. You could even reimagine the special ability they have to fit your own concept.*

For example, Big Drogg Fort-kicka's 'Grievous Halitosis' rule could be attributed to the fact your Mega-Gargant has the rotting corpse of a king's prized stallion strapped to his hip as a trophy. One-eyed Grunnock's 'Shake the Earth' ability could be attributed not to your Warstomper jumping up and down, but to their habit of belly-flopping the enemy army. Similarly, Bundo Whalebiter's 'Dead Cunning, for a Gargant' rule could be attributed not to the intellect-boosting effects of a stolen aelven artefact, but to the fact he has an 'advisor' from your army riding upon his shoulder. The only limit is your imagination!

BUNDO WHALEBITER – KRAKEN-EATER MERCENARY

If you pick this Mega-Gargant mercenary to be hired by your army, you must include 1 KRAKEN-EATER MEGA-GARGANT in your army as a MERCENARY unit.

KRAKEN-EATER MEGA-GARGANTS can only be taken as MERCENARY units by Order and Destruction armies, or by armies from factions that are part of the Order or Destruction Grand Alliance.

DEAD CUNNING, FOR A GARGANT

The aelven artefact hanging from Bundo's ear has increased his intellect, giving him brains as well as brawn. He can be uncannily patient, knowing just where and when to strike to cause maximum havoc. Some say his hoard even contains strange papery things called 'books'…

At the start of the combat phase, you can say that this model will be uncannily cunning. If you do so, this model fights at the end of that phase, but you can re-roll hit rolls for attacks made by this model in that phase.

In terms of raw power, the Hammerhalian expedition's greatest asset is the gargant they call 'Whalebiter'. This mountain of muscle talks to its manling paymasters in full sentences, though with enough growling and grunting to put a tundra walrus to shame. I even heard it use the phrase 'not the spirit of the deal', though it spat a bathload of spittle in doing so, and I swear a fish head fell out of its mouth.

In battle, the brute watches its enemies closely. It seems to learn as it fights, dismissing minor threats the better to slay the genuine danger. Grungni's beard, but I find that to be most disconcerting.

I suspect there has been some manner of enchantment lain upon the beast. Those aethermatic readings I have taken whilst it slumbers off its grog-binges certainly indicate some magical influence. Perhaps it is the work of those Collegiate dabblers, or even the aelves. I would not put it past the spike-eared prigs to unleash such a horror on the realms.

Though the creature has no love for Sigmar's stormlings, and though it looks at us Kharadron askance, it seems to have no grudge against our kind. Good thing too, given that the beast has reach enough to pull a Frigate from the skies. Thank the Code he's fighting on our side.

I must admit, I am looking forward to the coming battles against the horned umgi rather more than usual. They think they have the monopoly on linebreakers, those ones, with their Chimeras and tentacled terrors and the like. We'll see how clever they are when the Whalebiter gets in amongst them.

Nothing lasts forever, of course. I know it would be poor form to begin a sweepstake as to how long the big lug lasts before he bites off more than he can chew, or before we have to put him down with cannon fire from afar. But by Ironsson's purse, it's making my fingers itch even now.

- Almanac of Warrant Officer Kjardon Threebarrel, fourth mark, third week after Hammerhalian Skytake

ONE-EYED GRUNNOCK – WARSTOMPER MERCENARY

If you pick this Mega-Gargant mercenary to be hired by your army, you must include 1 **Warstomper Mega-Gargant** in your army as a **Mercenary** unit.

Warstomper Mega-Gargants can only be taken as **Mercenary** units by Chaos and Destruction armies, or by armies from factions that are part of the Chaos or Destruction Grand Alliance.

SHAKE THE EARTH

Grunnock has learned that the best way to break an enemy army is to shatter its cohesion. His signature move – leaping high before stomping down to cause a small earthquake – is feared for good reason.

You can re-roll hit rolls of 1 for Jump Up and Down attacks made by this model. In addition, subtract 1 from hit rolls for attacks made by enemy units that are within 6" of this model if this model made any Jump Up and Down attacks earlier in the same phase.

*Y*ou will have heard by now, great master, of the warp-machine. And yes-yes, what the Clanrats whisper is true. The lightning-vault was opened at my hand. Mine-mine, and mine alone! I, great and powerful Clawlord Rikkisquit, broke open the prison that the God-King had sealed. Though it was the One-eyed Giant that worked as my puppet. Big, big puppet. It was my genius that saw the deal made with the ironclad humans. I sent them to their deaths, and prevailed!

You should have seen it, master. Stronger than a Great Beast of Skavenskrol. More-more deadly than a thousand Stormvermin. It split the lightning-vault with a blow from its club, yes-yes. Broke the stone. Broke duardin stone, master, with one blow. The things that spilled out, much kill-kill in those ones. Little cog-scarabs with knives for legs. They fell on the idiot humans, lacerating, slash-slash. Much blood, rivers of blood, nostril-twitching and hot. We, the cunning ones, we waited. Only moved in once the kill-scarabs were stamped flat. The One-eye, he jumped, he stamped, he jumped again. Cogs everywhere. Death everywhere. All close by, knocked over. Clawlord Burriktak, he squirted the musk of fear. Squirted like always. Coward. I was brave. I charged in to kill a scarab with my blade, then another, then a hundred hundred thousand! So bold. Huge metal scream came from the vault door. Ears hurt bad then. Cog golem came out, hissing steam. One-eyed Giant smashed it, smashed it up. Imagine that strength against Skryre-clans!

We saw your warp-machine then, in the dark. So close. Yes-yes, it too was smashed. Not my fault. Gargant's fault. Lumber-ox stood on it in fight, broke it, no repair. Broke into shards. But it is not bad! A great victory! Those shards, those warpstone shards, they pierced One-eye's foot. They drive him mad, over time. They mutate him, over time. Then, when he is hungry for more, we will take him. Far better weapon than warp-machine. You will see-see. Trust me, master. I am the real giant!

BIG DROGG FORT-KICKA – GATEBREAKER MERCENARY

If you pick this Mega-Gargant mercenary to be hired by your army, you must include 1 **GATEBREAKER MEGA-GARGANT** in your army as a **MERCENARY** unit.

GATEBREAKER MEGA-GARGANTS can only be taken as **MERCENARY** units by Death and Destruction armies, or by armies from factions that are part of the Death or Destruction Grand Alliance.

GRIEVOUS HALITOSIS

Drogg has dined well on the spoils of war, having smashed and eaten the contents of many a fortified town – yet he has never picked his teeth clean. His breath is so foul it can stun an ox at ten paces.

At the end of the combat phase, you can pick 1 enemy unit within 3" of this model and roll a number of dice equal to the number of models from that unit that are within 3" of this model. For each 6, that unit suffers 1 mortal wound.

*I*t began as happenstance, my lady. The creature seemed barely more than a scavenger, despite its immense size. Valentian's procession had relieved Narvehal of its citizenry – or rather their souls, just as he had promised after their betrayal so long ago. In his wake, the beast came close behind. It seemed content to demolish the buildings, stopping only to consume the physical remains of the fallen. In doing so it robbed me of the very corpses with which I had planned to replenish my own unliving servants. That angered me greatly, at first.

I had no wish to attack the brute and trigger a costly battle. It got ever closer to my temporary haven in the Narvehal library, feeding on the lifeless bodies left in the Craven King's wake. I noticed, over time, that it avoided the gheists that lingered there.

Binding the gheists to my service with the Danse Macabre you so graciously taught me, I climbed Narvehal's bellspire and rang the bell as long as it took to get the creature's attention. Shouting at the top of my voice, I brokered the deal; it took an act of supreme fortitude to do so, for the beast's breath smelled like a middenheap in high summer. The creature would take a full half of the corpse-harvest after each conquest, so long as it attacked the targets I nominated, and provided my gheists kept their distance. The brute proved instrumental in the disruption of the arcane defences of Addisport and Malenheim alike. Should its obedience waver, we shall see how it performs as a walking corpse.

Darak Lor, Gravemaster of Carstinia

Postscript – As you know from our shared history, mistress, I have a strong stomach, but whenever I deal with this beast I keep a kerchief soaked in Nuhlahmian perfume close to hand. Please send more.

• WARSCROLL •

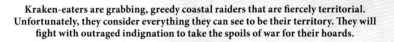

KRAKEN-EATER
MEGA-GARGANT

Kraken-eaters are grabbing, greedy coastal raiders that are fiercely territorial.
Unfortunately, they consider everything they can see to be their territory. They will
fight with outraged indignation to take the spoils of war for their hoards.

MISSILE WEAPONS	Range	Attacks	To Hit	To Wound	Rend	Damage
Hurled Debris	✸	3	4+	3+	-1	D3
MELEE WEAPONS	Range	Attacks	To Hit	To Wound	Rend	Damage
Almighty Stomp	2"	2	3+	3+	-2	D3
Death Grip	3"	1	3+	2+	-3	D6
Shipwrecka Warclub	3"	✸	3+	3+	-2	2

DAMAGE TABLE			
Wounds Suffered	Move	Shipwrecka Warclub	Hurled Debris
0-12	11"	8	24"
13-18	10"	7	21"
19-24	9"	7	18"
25-30	8"	6	15"
31+	7"	5	12"

DESCRIPTION

A Kraken-eater Mega-Gargant is a single model armed with an Almighty Stomp, Death Grip, Shipwrecka Warclub and Hurled Debris.

ABILITIES

Almighty Stomp: *A Mega-Gargant's massive, stomping feet are devastating against smaller opponents.*

You can re-roll hit rolls of 1 for Almighty Stomp attacks unless the target is a **Monster**.

Crushing Charge: *When a Mega-Gargant charges, its incredible bulk flattens any foe that fails to get out of the way.*

After this model makes a charge move, roll a dice for each enemy unit within 1" of this model. On a 2+, that unit suffers D3 mortal wounds if it is a **Monster**, or D6 mortal wounds if it is not a **Monster**.

Death Grip: *Mega-Gargants are perfectly capable of squeezing the life out of even the largest opponent.*

You can re-roll hit rolls of 1 for Death Grip attacks that target a **Monster**.

Get Orf Me Land!: *Kraken-eater Mega-Gargants hate intruders and trespassers, and do not take kindly to people that decide to fight battles on their land.*

In your hero phase, if you have any models with this ability within 1" of an objective that you control, you can pick one of those models and say that it will kick the objective away. If you do so, you can move that objective up to 2D6" to a new position on the battlefield, more than 1" away from any models, terrain features or other objectives. An objective cannot be kicked away more than once in the same phase.

Longshanks: *A Mega-Gargant towers high above the battlefield, and with its long powerful legs it can step over most obstacles.*

When this model makes a normal move, it can ignore models that have a Wounds characteristic of 10 or less and terrain features that are less than 4" tall at their highest point. It cannot finish the move on top of another model or within 3" of an enemy model.

Son of Behemat: *The Sons of Behemat are nearly as difficult to kill as their mighty progenitor.*

If a spell or ability would slay this model without any wounds or mortal wounds being inflicted by the spell or ability, this model suffers D6 mortal wounds instead.

Stuff 'Em In Me Net: *Kraken-eaters are constantly putting things into the nets they carry 'for later', including unlucky opponents and other tasty-looking morsels.*

After this model piles in, you can pick up to D3 enemy models within 3" of this model and roll a dice for each of them. If the roll is at least double that model's Wounds characteristic, it is slain.

Terror: *This terrifying monstrosity strikes fear into the hearts of its foes.*

Subtract 1 from the Bravery characteristic of enemy units if they are within 3" of any friendly units with this ability.

Timberrrrr!: *A dying Mega-Gargant is a weapon of ruin in its own right, though it is anyone's guess where – and on whom – their body falls.*

If this model is slain, before removing the model from the battlefield, the players must roll off. The winner must pick a point on the battlefield 5" from this model. Each unit within 3" of that point suffers D3 mortal wounds unless it is a **Mega-Gargant**. This model is then removed from the battlefield.

KEYWORDS	DESTRUCTION, SONS OF BEHEMAT, GARGANT, MEGA-GARGANT, MONSTER, HERO, KRAKEN-EATER

WARSTOMPER
MEGA-GARGANT

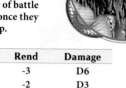

MOVE 35 | **SAVE** 4+ | **BRAVERY** 7 | **WOUNDS**

The veteran warmongers of the gargant race seek out the thrill and clangour of battle wherever they can find it. They love smashing battlelines into disarray, and once they are in the thick of the fight, their rampage is all but impossible to stop.

MELEE WEAPONS	Range	Attacks	To Hit	To Wound	Rend	Damage
Death Grip	3"	1	3+	2+	-3	D6
Jump Up and Down	3"	4	3+	3+	-2	D3
Titanic Boulderclub	3"	✸	3+	3+	-2	2

DAMAGE TABLE			
Wounds Suffered	Move	Titanic Boulderclub	Hurled Body
0-12	10"	+4	+2
13-18	9"	+3	+1
19-24	8"	+2	0
25-30	7"	+1	-1
31+	6"	0	-2

DESCRIPTION

A Warstomper Mega-Gargant is a single model armed with a Death Grip, Jump Up and Down and Titanic Boulderclub.

ABILITIES

Almighty Jump: *A Mega-Gargant's massive, stomping feet are devastating against smaller opponents.*

You can re-roll hit rolls of 1 for Jump Up and Down attacks unless the target is a **MONSTER**.

Crushing Charge: *When a Mega-Gargant charges, its incredible bulk flattens any foe that fails to get out of the way.*

After this model makes a charge move, roll a dice for each enemy unit within 1" of this model. On a 2+, that unit suffers D3 mortal wounds if it is a **MONSTER**, or D6 mortal wounds if it is not a **MONSTER**.

Death Grip: *Mega-Gargants are perfectly capable of squeezing the life out of even the largest opponent.*

You can re-roll hit rolls of 1 for Death Grip attacks that target a **MONSTER**.

Hurled Body: *Warstomper Mega-Gargants wade into the thick of battle, and will pick up smaller opponents to hurl at other enemies.*

Once per combat phase, you can pick 1 enemy model within 3" of this model and roll a dice. Add the Hurled Body modifier shown on this model's damage table to the roll. If the roll is at least double that enemy model's Wounds characteristic, it is slain and you can roll another dice. On a 4+, you can pick an enemy unit within 12" of this model and visible to it. That unit suffers a number of mortal wounds equal to the Wounds characteristic of the slain model.

Longshanks: *A Mega-Gargant towers high above the battlefield, and with its long powerful legs it can step over most obstacles.*

When this model makes a normal move, it can ignore models that have a Wounds characteristic of 10 or less and terrain features that are less than 4" tall at their highest point. It cannot finish the move on top of another model or within 3" of an enemy model.

Son of Behemat: *The Sons of Behemat are nearly as difficult to kill as their mighty progenitor.*

If a spell or ability would slay this model without any wounds or mortal wounds being inflicted by the spell or ability, this model suffers D6 mortal wounds instead.

Terror: *This terrifying monstrosity strikes fear into the hearts of its foes.*

Subtract 1 from the Bravery characteristic of enemy units if they are within 3" of any friendly units with this ability.

Timberrrrr!: *A dying Mega-Gargant is a weapon of ruin in its own right, though it is anyone's guess where – and on whom – their body falls.*

If this model is slain, before removing the model from the battlefield, the players must roll off. The winner must pick a point on the battlefield 5" from this model. Each unit within 3" of that point suffers D3 mortal wounds unless it is a **MEGA-GARGANT**. This model is then removed from the battlefield.

Titanic Boulderclub: *A Warstomper Mega-Gargant will drive straight into the midst of the foe, swinging their titanic boulderclub in great sweeping arcs that smash foes in all directions.*

The Attacks characteristic of a Titanic Boulderclub is equal to the number of enemy models within 3" of the attacking model. Add the Titanic Boulderclub value on the attacking model's damage table to the total, and add 4 to the total for each enemy **MONSTER** within 3" of the attacking model. If the modified Attacks characteristic of the Titanic Boulderclub is less than 1, count it as being 1, and if the modified Attacks characteristic of the Titanic Boulderclub is more than 10, count it as being 10.

KEYWORDS	DESTRUCTION, SONS OF BEHEMAT, GARGANT, MEGA-GARGANT, MONSTER, HERO, WARSTOMPER

78

MOVE
WOUNDS 35 | 4+ SAVE
7
BRAVERY

GATEBREAKER
MEGA-GARGANT

Cowled and sinister, the Gatebreaker is a wrecking ball of a gargant that takes cruel joy in smashing down the fortresses and cities of the civilised races before throwing the rubble at any survivors. To him, every structure is a target for his spiteful wrath.

MISSILE WEAPONS	Range	Attacks	To Hit	To Wound	Rend	Damage
Hurled Boulder	✸	1	3+	2+	-3	4
MELEE WEAPONS	Range	Attacks	To Hit	To Wound	Rend	Damage
Almighty Stomp	2"	2	3+	3+	-2	D3
Death Grip	3"	1	3+	2+	-3	D6
Fortcrusha Flail	3"	✸	4+	3+	-3	3

DAMAGE TABLE				
Wounds Suffered	Move	Fortcrusha Flail	Hurled Boulder	Smash Down
0-12	12"	10	18"	2+
13-18	11"	9	15"	3+
19-24	10"	7	12"	4+
25-30	9"	6	9"	5+
31+	8"	5	6"	6+

DESCRIPTION

A Gatebreaker Mega-Gargant is a single model armed with an Almighty Stomp, Death Grip, Fortcrusha Flail and Hurled Boulder.

ABILITIES

Almighty Stomp: *A Mega-Gargant's massive, stomping feet are devastating against smaller opponents.*

You can re-roll hit rolls of 1 for Almighty Stomp attacks unless the target is a **MONSTER**.

Crushing Charge: *When a Mega-Gargant charges, its incredible bulk flattens any foe that fails to get out of the way.*

After this model makes a charge move, roll a dice for each enemy unit within 1" of this model. On a 2+, that unit suffers D3 mortal wounds if it is a **MONSTER**, or D6 mortal wounds if it is not a **MONSTER**.

Death Grip: *Mega-Gargants are perfectly capable of squeezing the life out of even the largest opponent.*

You can re-roll hit rolls of 1 for Death Grip attacks that target a **MONSTER**.

Longshanks: *A Mega-Gargant towers high above the battlefield, and with its long powerful legs it can step over most obstacles.*

When this model makes a normal move, it can ignore models that have a Wounds characteristic of 10 or less and terrain features that are less than 4" tall at their highest point. It cannot finish the move on top of another model or within 3" of an enemy model.

Smash Down: *Gatebreaker Mega-Gargants have a deep loathing of cities and settlements, which are seen as symbols of those who killed their ancestor figure, the godbeast Behemat.*

Add 1 to the damage inflicted by each successful attack made by this model that targets a unit that is part of a garrison or is wholly on or within a terrain feature.

In addition, at the end of the combat phase, you can pick 1 terrain feature within 3" of this model and roll a dice. If the roll is equal to or greater than the Smash Down value on this model's damage table, that terrain feature is reduced to rubble: all of its scenery rules are replaced with the Deadly scenery rule, and its keywords are changed to **SCENERY, RUBBLE**.

Son of Behemat: *The Sons of Behemat are nearly as difficult to kill as their mighty progenitor.*

If a spell or ability would slay this model without any wounds or mortal wounds being inflicted by the spell or ability, this model suffers D6 mortal wounds instead.

Terror: *This terrifying monstrosity strikes fear into the hearts of its foes.*

Subtract 1 from the Bravery characteristic of enemy units if they are within 3" of any friendly units with this ability.

Timberrrrr!: *A dying Mega-Gargant is a weapon of ruin in its own right, though it is anyone's guess where – and on whom – their body falls.*

If this model is slain, before removing the model from the battlefield, the players must roll off. The winner must pick a point on the battlefield 5" from this model. Each unit within 3" of that point suffers D3 mortal wounds, unless it is a **MEGA-GARGANT**. This model is then removed from the battlefield.

KEYWORDS	DESTRUCTION, SONS OF BEHEMAT, GARGANT, MEGA-GARGANT, MONSTER, HERO, GATEBREAKER

MANCRUSHER GARGANTS

MOVE 8"
WOUNDS 12
SAVE 5+
BRAVERY 7

When the earth shakes to the thunder of the Mega-Gargants' footfalls, their lesser brethren muster for war. No longer are they aimless nomads and indulgent drunkards, but war-hungry terrors inspired to violence by their towering brethren.

MELEE WEAPONS	Range	Attacks	To Hit	To Wound	Rend	Damage
'Eadbutt	1"	1	4+	3+	-3	✹
Massive Club	3"	✹	3+	3+	-1	1
Mighty Kick	2"	1	3+	3+	-2	D3

DAMAGE TABLE			
Wounds Suffered	Stomping Charge	Massive Club	'Eadbutt
0-2	2+	10	4
3-4	3+	9	3
5-7	4+	8	3
8-9	5+	6	2
10+	6+	4	1

DESCRIPTION

A unit of Mancrusher Gargants has any number of models, each armed with an 'Eadbutt, Massive Club and Mighty Kick.

ABILITIES

Keep Up!: *Mancrusher Gargants run along as fast as they can, so as not to be left behind when their bigger brethren charge into battle.*

If this unit is within 12" of a friendly **MEGA-GARGANT** at the start of the charge phase, it can attempt to charge in that charge phase even if it ran in the same turn.

Stomping Charge: *When a Mancrusher Gargant charges, it smashes into the foe with the unstoppable force of an avalanche.*

After a model from this unit makes a charge move, pick 1 enemy unit within 1" of it and roll a dice. If the roll is equal to or greater than the Stomping Charge value for the charging model shown on the damage table above, that unit suffers D3 mortal wounds. If this unit has more than 1 model, do not allocate the mortal wounds until all of the models in this unit have made their charge moves.

Stuff 'Em In Me Bag: *Gargants are known to grab hapless warriors and stuff them screaming into their bags 'for later'…*

After a model from this unit piles in, you can pick 1 enemy model within 3" of it and roll a dice. If the roll is at least double that model's Wounds characteristic, it is slain.

Timber!: *A dying gargant is a weapon of ruin in its own right, though it is anyone's guess where – and on whom – their body falls.*

If a model from this unit is slain, before removing it from the battlefield, the players must roll off. The winner must pick a point on the battlefield 3" from that model. Each unit within 2" of that point suffers D3 mortal wounds unless it is a **GARGANT**. The model is then removed from the battlefield.

KEYWORDS	DESTRUCTION, SONS OF BEHEMAT, GARGANT, MONSTER, MANCRUSHER

PITCHED BATTLE PROFILES

The table below provides points, minimum and maximum unit sizes and battlefield roles for the warscrolls and warscroll battalions in this book, for use in Pitched Battles. Spending the points listed in this table allows you to take a minimum-sized unit with any of its upgrades. Understrength units cost the full amount of points. Larger units are taken in multiples of their minimum unit size; multiply their cost by the same amount as you multiplied their size. If a unit has two points values separated by a slash (e.g. '60/200'), the second value is for a maximum-sized unit. Units that are listed as 'Unique' are named characters and can only be taken once in an army. A unit that has any of the keywords listed on the Allies table can be taken as an allied unit by a Sons of Behemat army. Updated April 2020; the profiles printed here take precedence over any profiles with an earlier publication date or no publication date.

SONS OF BEHEMAT WARSCROLL	UNIT SIZE MIN	UNIT SIZE MAX	POINTS	BATTLEFIELD ROLE	NOTES
Mancrusher Gargants	1	3	180/480	Behemoth	In a Sons of Behemat army, battlefield role is Battleline (not Behemoth) and maximum-sized units count as 3 Battleline units.
Gatebreaker Mega-Gargant	1	1	490	Leader, Behemoth	
Kraken-eater Mega-Gargant	1	1	490	Leader, Behemoth	
Warstomper Mega-Gargant	1	1	480	Leader, Behemoth	

FACTION	ALLIES
Sons of Behemat	None

*O*lag sat deep in his cave, slow thoughts sliding like icebergs in the dark waters of his mind. He closed his good eye for a moment and listened hard, his forearms on his knees and his back flat against the wall where the strange paintings appeared as he slept. Sometimes, the night before a big fight, pictures appeared on his skin, too. Patterns of red, white and black. His hair got twisted all regular at night, sometimes, and he heard skittering and scuffling on the cusp of hearing as he woke.

He'd given up getting angry about it, given up punching the cave walls in frustration that someone or something was messing with him whilst he slept. It was the Creepers that did it, those pale, dirty little stick-figures that always kept just out of sight. Stick-figures, like on the walls. Sometimes he heard them whisper-singing, in the tunnels, or saw torchlight glinting from eyes in the dark. 'Olag. Olag. Olag the Great,' they chanted in their weird, hollow voices. It wasn't so bad, especially when they left him food. They could stay, he thought, so long as they stayed well out of sight.

Sighing heavily, Olag got up slowly, his old joints creaking like oaks in a storm. The moon outside the cave was fat, and that meant he had a meet to keep.

***

The human runts were lined up all neat on their stupid cliff-road, the dawn sun glinting from their shiny bits. Idiots, thought Olag. That just made them easier to kill. He broke into a run, and planted his best foot right in the middle of one of the formations. It hurt his foot, but it hurt the runts far more. He felt humans bursting, sticky and wet. Chuckling, Olag

took another step towards the cliff, shaking the corpses from his toes as he swept his club backhand into one of the squawking lion-birds the human lords like to ride. It broke the beast with a satisfying crunch. He felt stinging bites on his back, and turned to see another group of humans, smoke rising from their fire-sticks. Roaring, he kicked half of them over the cliff edge into the sea. Then he heard the sound of horse-riders charging in, their pointy things levelled. Too late to get out of the way, thought Olag. This was going to hurt.

A massive net flew over the clifftop, falling on the riders and dragging them, horses and all, over the edge. A moment later, Salty Borag's ugly, toothless face loomed into sight, brine cascading from his wrinkled brown arm as he reached out over the cliff to sweep another dozen humans into the sea.

Olag laughed, long and loud, and stamped another knot of humans into mush. At times like this, he felt good. He was a king, and all was right with the world.

***

Back at his cave, Olag poked at the wound in his knee, wincing as the Creepers dug the sting-rocks out of his back. He could hear them whispering, feel their ropes tugging his mantle back into place, even feel their feet on his skin. He let it slide. They would sew up his wounds after a fight, just as they did his rags. The cave stank of blood; they would be busy for a while. He still felt good, even though he had taken a fair few hits.

Not as many as that heavy old git Borag, he thought, idly snapping off a finger from the sea giant's cadaver. Took a while to haul him back, but it was worth it. They would eat well that night, Creepers and all.